Emily

EVENTING

EVENTING

SHEILA ROUGHTON BHSI

WARD LOCK

A WARD LOCK BOOK

First published in the UK 1993
by Ward Lock
A Cassell Imprint
Villiers House
41/47 Strand
LONDON
WC2N 5JE

Distributed in the United States
by Sterling Publishing Co., Inc.
387 Park Avenue South, New York, NY 10016-8810

Distributed in Australia
by Capricorn Link (Australia) Pty Ltd
P.O. Box 665, Lane Cove, NSW 2066

British Library Cataloguing in Publication Data
The CIP data for this book is available
upon application to the British Library

ISBN 0-7063-7125-9

Typeset in Monophoto Goudy Old Style
by Litho Link Ltd, Welshpool, Powys, Wales

All photographs by Equestrian Services Thorney

Printed and bound in Great Britain by Hillmans (Frome) Ltd

Frontispiece: Prizegiving at Burghley

CONTENTS

THE AUTHOR

SHEILA ROUGHTON has many years' experience of training both horses and riders. She has competed at all levels and is a BHS Chief Examiner and currently a full time lecturer at Moulton College, Northampton. She has recently turned her hand to writing and from first hand experience has produced several practical books, aimed at riders of all levels.

ACKNOWLEDGEMENTS

My thanks must go to all the people and horses who made the writing of this book possible: especially to my father, Geoffrey Chandler, firstly for his help in training and making it possible for me to start my eventing career and secondly for encouraging me to write about it and then adding the vital pieces of information I had forgotten!

Also to Mary Cheney who, as always, has spent many hours typing the text, and to Ian and Martha Shaw for their photographs.

The author and publishers would like to thank the British Horse Society Horse Trials Group for permission to quote from the Horse Trials Rule Book.

Riders should be aware of all current rules and take note that the Rule Book is updated annually and anyone competing in Horse Trials should study this thoroughly beforehand.

The BHS Horse Trials Group is not responsible for any errors or omissions contained in this book.

INTRODUCTION

Eventing is an addiction – once hooked it is almost impossible to give up! Although at times, when you have risen at the crack of dawn and are driving down the motorway in the pouring rain, you may ask yourself why on earth are you doing it, you will soon know the answer when the sun shines and your horse performs beyond your wildest dreams.

There is no easy way to keep and ride an event horse, even if you do not work full-time and have generous financial means. Anyone wishing to compete must have the determination to succeed and this is only achieved by being prepared to put in extra hours of work on top of your normal employment and to forego other pleasures like a full social life and expensive material goods. Right at the beginning, I must also mention the need to have a long-suffering helper without whom none of us could ever manage!

Eventing in Great Britain is such a rapidly growing activity that it is hard to remember its history as a popular sport in this country is comparatively recent. It is also ironic that we remain the leading nation in a sport that we imported when we have been overtaken by other countries in sports we invented, for example cricket and football.

The sport of horse trials originated in Europe in the form of a three-day event known as 'the military', a title that still lingers in some other European countries. Switzerland can fairly claim to have run the first one-day horse trials in 1922. There is some disagreement as to the exact date on which the first one-day event was held in Britain, although it seems fairly certain that it was at Wellsbourne in 1946. Badminton was held for the first time in 1949, with the British Horse Society providing the prize money of twenty pounds for the winner! It was at this time that interest in such competitions began to grow.

The training of the event horse is the most complete of all equine disciplines. It requires extreme fitness in the horse, which must produce a calm, relaxed performance in the dressage, followed by speed and courage across country and then obedience and accuracy in the show jumping. This not only requires a thorough all-round training for the horse but also the establishment of a strong bond of trust between mount and rider. One of the attractions of the sport is the opportunity it gives us to experience and enjoy that special pleasure that is found in the partnership of rider and horse. It has frequently been said that 'To travel hopefully is better than to arrive'. Obviously, to arrive is the best outcome, but travelling hopefully can also be extremely rewarding during training.

Another great bonus of this sport is the wonderful places in which competitions are staged. Many are held in the beautiful parks surrounding large country houses, providing an opportunity for everyone to enjoy their splendour. Whether they are held in these magnificent surroundings or in an ordinary field the atmosphere is unique. It is the camaraderie among competitors which forms the main attraction of eventing. In horse trials there is always a helping hand available, even from fellow competitors, in the case of misfortune or disaster.

CHAPTER ONE

THE EVENTING LADDER

The pleasure of eventing can be enjoyed by riders at all levels once a certain level of proficiency has been reached. The best starting point for the younger rider is the Pony Club, which provides an excellent introduction to all aspects of equestrianism, including horse trials. Within the various Pony Club branches novice and open classes are held, with expert advice on hand if required. For more proficient riders there is the opportunity of riding in teams representing each branch at area competitions. The winners of these then qualify for the National Championships. Most of the top British riders started in the Pony Club and then progressed to the junior selection trials which are open to riders between the ages of fifteen and eighteen. After the experience gained as a junior, or for anyone wanting to enter the sport between the ages of nineteen and 21, there is the facility known as Young Riders.

For adults the starting point is probably a local Riding Club, which is in many ways an adult version of the Pony Club. This will provide an introduction to horse trials, with the opportunity to ride later in teams and even at a National Championship.

The British Horse Society is the governing body regarding horse trials

and all horses and riders have to be registered members of the BHS before being eligible to enter BHS-run events. The beginning of the BHS scale starts with Pre-Novice but before competing at this level both horse and rider should be capable of being placed in open Pony Club or Riding Club events.

Grading of Horses

In all official horse trials, including those restricted to Young Riders but excluding those confined to Juniors and Pre-Novice classes, points are awarded to horses according to their placing and the number of starters in the dressage. At present, the grade of a horse is determined as follows:

Grade 1	61 or more points
Grade 2	from 21 to 61 points
Grade 3	less than 21 points
Ungraded	horses only registered for Pre-Novice

The owners of the horse must keep a record of how many points their horse has won.

Riding Club Competition

Grading list, showing how points are accumulated

One-Day Horse Trials

Novice/Open Novice			Intermediate/ Open Intermediate	Advanced
Place	Starters	Points	Points	Points
1		6	12	24
2		5	10	22
3		4	8	20
4	Over 15	3	6	18
5	Over 19	2	4	16
6	Over 23	1	2	14
7	Over 27	1	2	12
8	Over 31	1	2	10

Two- and three-day events have a larger number of points.

CLASSES

Pre-Novice designed to encourage novice horses and/or riders by offering lower fences at slower speeds. They are open to ungraded horses and those without points.

Novice restricted to Grade 3 horses.

Open Novice restricted to Grade 2 horses with less than 36 points and to Grade 3 horses. The dressage and show jumping is at Intermediate standard and the cross-country is at Novice standard.

Intermediate restricted to Grade 2 and Grade 3 horses.

Open Intermediate open to all grades. This class is at Intermediate standard.

Advanced restricted to Grade 1 and Grade 2 horses.

SUMMARY

1. Eventing can be enjoyed by riders at all levels.
2. Valuable experience may be gained at unaffiliated horse trials.
3. At affiliated competitions, points are awarded to horses according to their placing.
4. The classes start with Pre-Novice for novice horses and/or riders and go through various other stages to Advanced.

CHAPTER TWO

WHAT ARE HORSE TRIALS?

The terms 'eventing' and 'horse trials' are synonymous. The general trend nowadays is towards calling the sport 'horse trials', although participating horses will probably always be called eventers.

Basically, horse trials test the ability of horse and rider in their performance of dressage, cross-country and show jumping. In two- and three-day trials, additional tests are introduced to cover ability to ride roads and tracks in a disciplined manner and to perform over steeplechase fences at a fast speed. Throughout the speed and endurance phase, time is all important.

In each test penalty marks are awarded for mistakes made by the horse and rider, and these are cumulative. The competitor who finishes the whole test with the least amount of penalty points is the winner.

THE DRESSAGE TEST

The influence of the dressage phase on the overall result is becoming increasingly more important as riders strive to improve their general standard. Gone are the days when a good cross-country horse could still win despite a mediocre score in the dressage. That said, the most influential phase of all will always be the ability to ride clear over the cross-country course within the allocated time.

The dressage test is ridden from memory in a standard 20 × 40-m arena, up to and including Intermediate standard. A larger arena, of 20 × 60 m, is normally used for Advanced classes.

A 20 × 40-m dressage arena

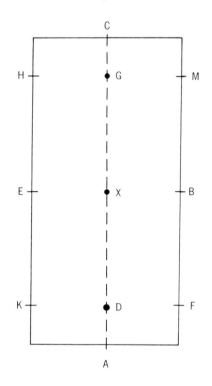

Sample Novice Dressage Test

THE BRITISH HORSE SOCIETY'S
HORSE TRIALS DRESSAGE TEST B (1979)
Approximate Time - 4 mins
(Novice Standard)

To be ridden in a snaffle bridle   Max. marks

1.	A	Enter at working trot	
	X	Halt. Salute. Proceed at working trot	10
2.	C	Track left	10
3.	A	Working trot half circle left 20m diameter	
	X	Half circle right 20m diameter	10
4.	CM	Working trot	
	MXK	Change rein showing a few lengthened strides	10
5.	K	Working trot	
	FXH	Change rein showing a few lengthened strides	10
6.	C	Working canter	
	B	Circle right 20m diameter	
	BF	Working canter	10
7.	F	Working trot	
	A	Medium walk	
	KB	Change rein at free walk on a long rein	
	BM	Medium walk	10
8.	M	Working trot	
		Between	
	C&H	Working canter	
	E	Circle left 20m diameter	
	EK	Working canter	10
9.	K	Working trot	
	A	Down centre line	
	G	Halt. Salute	10
		Leave arena at walk on a long rein at A	
10.		General impression, obedience and calmness	10
11.		Paces (freedom & regularity) and impulsion	10
12.		Position and seat of the rider and correct application of the aids	10

Arena 20m x 40m   TOTAL 120

N.B. In B.H.S. & Horse Trials NOVICE TESTS, trot work may be executed either "sitting" or "rising" at the discretion of the rider.

Saddlery and Equipment allowed for Horse Trials

	Ordinary Snaffle	Simple Double Bridle	Whip	Gloves and Spurs	Flash/ Grakle/ Drop Noseband	Bit Guards
Novice	√	x	x	Comp.	√	x
Intermediate	√	√	x	Comp.	√	x
Advanced	√	√	x	Comp.	√	x

Martingales and boots are not permitted for dressage.   Comp. = compulsory

The judges are positioned at the C end of the arena and have a printed sheet of the test to be ridden in front of them. They will award marks from nought to ten for each numbered movement and for each of the collective marks at the end. These marks are then added together and the total marks are subtracted from the maximum number obtainable. To convert good marks into penalties, a coefficient is then applied that will

Dimensions of Show Jumping Obstacles

	Maximum Height	Maximum Spread
Pre-Novice	1.10 m (3'7") at highest point	1.20 m (3'11")
	at base	2.15 m (7'0)
Novice and all normal Junior classes	1.15 m (3'9") at highest point	1.20 m (3'11")
	at base	2.15 m (7')
Intermediate, Open Intermediate, Junior O.1. classes	1.20 m (3'11") at highest point	1.50 m (4'11")
	at base	2.45 m (8')
	water	2.60 m (8'6")
Advanced	1.25 m (4'1") at highest point	1.80 m (5'11")
	at base	2.80 m (9'2")
	water	3.00 m (9'10")

Penalties Awarded in the Show Jumping

Knockdown	5 penalties
Foot in the water or on tape	5 penalties
First disobedience	10 penalties
Second disobedience in whole test	20 penalties
Third disobedience in whole test	elimination
Fall of horse/rider	30 penalties

vary according to the particular test being used in order to guard against the dressage score having a disproportionate influence on the final result. Any error will be penalised as follows:

1st time – 2 marks
2nd time – 4 marks
3rd time – 8 marks
4th time – elimination

The test is designed to show the obedience of the horse even though it is also fit enough to run for its life. The movements must be performed with freedom and regularity in all paces and with elasticity of action. The horse must show a willingness to move forward, with true engagement of the hindquarters, but also be attentive and accept the bridle.

ONE-DAY EVENT

The next phase at a one-day event is generally the show jumping. The course will not ask the horse any more difficult questions than the cross-country but it still has to be treated with great respect. A knock down or a carelessly ridden turn can greatly influence the final result. Hours are spent in training to reduce the dressage score by one or two marks so it is silly to incur penalties in this phase through lack of concentration.

Horses must be trained over coloured fences including fillers and gymnastic jumping can be beneficial. Horses that are going to compete at a BHS Novice event must be capable of jumping a Newcomers course happily and comfortably before entering. Riders should also have experience at the same level and, as with all show jumping, the course should be walked properly before the competition starts. This is explained in more detail on pages 55–56.

At a one-day trial the cross-country is generally the last phase to be completed. No roads or tracks nor a steeplechase phase will be involved. The test consists purely of a number of cross-country obstacles, varying between fourteen for Pre-Novice and 30 for Advanced classes, to be completed at a specified speed. The speed increases the higher up the scale the competitiom is rated.

THREE-DAY EVENT

At a three-day event the first day is given over to dressage and the second day is devoted entirely to speed and endurance, which includes two phases of roads and tracks, steeplechase fences and a cross-country course.

1. Phases A and C (Roads and Tracks) These two phases are ridden

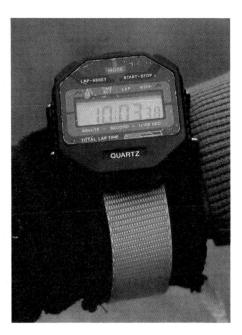

Digital stop-watch

over natural terrain over a stipulated distance at a stipulated speed. No jumps are involved. The course is marked off in kilometres and it is the responsibility of the competitor to keep to the times that have been worked out after walking the course prior to riding it. Each kilometre should take four minutes, except in the case of bad terrain or at the end of the steeplechase section where the horse will obviously need a short time to recover. If any walking is done, it becomes imperative to do some canter to catch up the time. Generally a good trot with a little cantering will be sufficient. Gauging the correct speed depends on the type of horse and which pace takes less out of him. Having aimed at four minutes per kilometre there should be a couple of minutes in hand to check the horse's equipment before setting

Horse and rider on the steeplechase course at a three-day event

off on the steeplechase phase.

There is no reward for completing these phases in less than the optimum time, but a competitor who exceeds the optimum time will be penalised by one penalty point for each second over the optimum time.

2. Phase B (Steeplechase) This is ridden over a predetermined distance with a number of steeplechase fences

to be jumped within a designated time. The competitor is penalised 0.8 of a penalty point for each second in excess of the optimum time. Again, there is no advantage to be gained from completing the course faster than the optimum time.

3. Phase D (Cross-Country) Again this is a measured distance with a variety of fences to be negotiated within the optimum time. Exceeding the optimum time in this section results in 0.4 of a penalty point for each second, in addition to any jumping penalties incurred on the way round.

Inspection of Horses

Before a horse is allowed even to start the competition at a three-day event, it has to pass a veterinary inspection, which is usually carried out on the day before the dressage begins. Later, between the second roads and tracks phase and the cross-country, there is a break of ten minutes and during this interval a committee, composed of one member of the Ground Jury and a veterinary surgeon and two judges, will examine each horse in order to decide whether it is fit to continue. Should they decide that a horse is

Horse being trotted up for the vet

The frenzied activity that takes place 'in the box' at a three-day event

unfit, they are responsible for ordering its immediate withdrawal.

This compulsory rest also affords an opportunity for the 'ground staff' to refresh both horse and rider, check saddlery and even, on occasions for emergency shoeing.

To satisfy the vets, the best ploy is for the competitor to approach the box at a steady trot in order to allay any suspicion of unsoundness in the horse.

The ten minutes spent in the box usually seems the shortest ten minutes in anybody's life. Frenzied activity takes place, with saddlery being removed, horses washed down and refreshed and the rider fortified with a swig of orange juice. Two minutes' warning is given by the stewards to be present on the Phase D

starting line and the clock starts whether you are there or not. Hence the frenzy!

Show Jumping
This phase takes place on the last day of a three-day event.

The test is ridden over a course containing ten to twelve obstacles and must be carried out at a specific speed. Completing the course in less than the time allowed is not rewarded but exceeding the time allowed is penalised by 0.25 of a penalty point for each second over the time.

Although the dimensions of the fences are less demanding than the top grades of show jumping, it must be borne in mind that the participating horses have already completed two days of competition which have made great demands on their physical endurance and gymnastic ability. Furthermore, up until now they have been encouraged to jump out of gallop in what tends to be a somewhat flattened bascule (the rounded shape made by the horse as it jumps). On the third day, however, they are required to jump accurately and with precision over closely sited obstacles requiring an entirely different flight pattern through the air. Time still plays an important part and much courage and endurance during the previous day's performance can come to nought for want of the odd second or two on the jumping round.

SUMMARY

1. Horse trials test the competitor in all three main disciplines: dressage, show jumping, cross-country. This is the complete test of the horse and rider.
2. The system of marking consists of penalty marks subtracted from a possible score in dressage and imposed for infringements in the other two phases. Both jumping and time penalties may be levied.
3. One-day events do not include roads and tracks or steeplechase and so are less demanding from an endurance point of view.

CHAPTER THREE

SELECTING THE RIGHT HORSE AND EQUIPMENT

THE HORSE

Horses come in all shapes and sizes so it is difficult, if not impossible, to give a precise definition of the perfect event horse. Such a creature is yet to be born, but it must be said that most of the top class performers do have good conformation which enables them to do the work asked of them comfortable and happily. Obviously, doing work that the horse finds easy will make the learning process more enjoyable. The other points that I consider to be of great importance are:

- soundness
- temperament
- natural ability
- type

Few horses are totally useless but there are many who need patience and understanding in their handling. When training any horse it is vital that the reason behind any problem that occurs is understood. It is this understanding that will differentiate between the good trainer and the bad. It must also be remembered that muscles and general fitness need time to develop and cannot be rushed.

Conformation

The ideal horse must be in proportion throughout, with the powerhouse of the quarters matching the scope of the forehand.

Seen sideways on, the horse should fill a square and have a leg firmly at each corner. As I have said, there are very few near perfect horses, but those that have a natural balance and are athletic in their movements have an obvious advantage. A pretty head and/or colour are purely cosmetic and should not be taken into consideration when assessing performance, although there is an old saying that the best horses have the head of a ladies maid and the bottom of a cook! Of course, an attractive appearance is always a bonus. Some horses have natural 'presence' which will develop further with correct training as the horse becomes more confident in its own ability and as its character evolves.

A sloping shoulder and big front are ideal for the show ring and for hunting as these features give riders confidence and make them feel they have a lot in front of them. This conformation is not ideal for the

Choosing a horse with good conformation is vital to achieving success

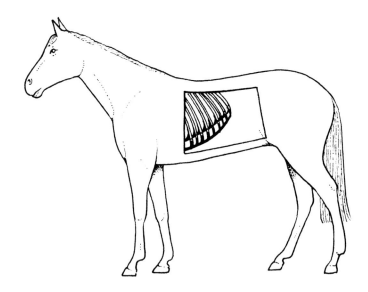

Being too long in the back will lead to weakness in the loin area

event horse, however, as it will find it difficult to rise over fences unless it has quarters to match. A horse with a huge frame can become cumbersome and lose its athleticism. There must be enough shoulder to allow freedom of movement and length of stride and also to give the agility to recover from a blunder over a fence. A good sloping shoulder can also give nice paces in the dressage arena.

The back must be long enough to enable the horse to do fast work and have the scope for a good length of stride and to jump big fences. Being too long in the back will lead to weakness in the area of the loins but too short a back will result in lack of scope and a choppy stride.

The hindleg is probably the most important component of the event horse, as it has to propel the horse forward, balance it, allow it to 'sit' back on its hocks and, of course, jump. It is also important when the need arises to shorten the stride or

convert a stride into a bounce. The leg needs to be long from the hip to the hock to give the horse enough leverage. When the horse is standing still, the point of the hock must be directly underneath the point of the buttock. A good jumper will always have a good hindleg and thus an event horse needs a good hindleg in order to jump and also to carry its weight back and lighten at the front.

The top outline of the horse should show prominence over the hip joints and then slope away to the dock. A rounded line in this area may be attractive for the show horse but it is inefficient with regard to the show jumper or the eventer. Look also for a fairly extensive length from the highest point of the quarters to the root of the dock. A prominent point here is known as a 'jumper's bump'.

There must be good width between the hips and an equal amount of muscle development on each side of the backbone. If the hindlegs appear

To be in good balance the horse must be capable of 'sitting back on its hocks'

to be bandy when looked at from behind, this usually denotes power. Cow hocks, showing the points of the hocks facing inwards, are the direct opposite of this and suggest that the hindlegs are weak.

The pasterns must not be too upright nor too long and sloping. An upright pastern can make the horse's stride rather short and choppy, which is uncomfortable for the rider and causes a lot of jarring to the horse. Long, sloping pasterns, although very comfortable for the rider, put enormous pressure on the tendons and can cause just as many veterinary problems as short, upright pasterns. Pasterns need to be halfway between the two extremes to give the steps some spring and give the horse a good

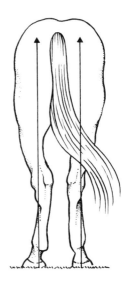

Cow hocks

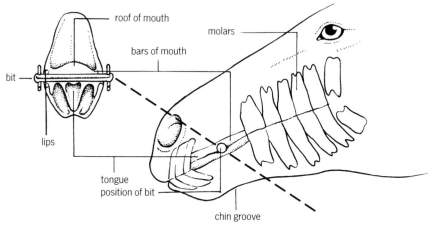

The shape of the jaw must allow the bit to fit comfortably in the mouth

length of stride. Most problems with the front legs are usually caused by upright shoulders and/or pasterns, foot problems, or by making too many demands of the horse when it is still physically immature. Horses should not begin training until they are four years old, despite the commercial pressures of the racing world. Many horses are not fully grown and properly balanced until they are seven years old! The aim throughout the training programme must be to get the horse's weight back onto its hocks so that the fore-legs, which are not designed to take too much strain, can be freed and the front of the horse can lighten.

How the head and neck are joined and how they are set on to the shoulders must also be considered. A horse that has a neck set too low on to the shoulders is never going to be able to work naturally in a correct shape. One with a bull neck is never going to be able to work on the bit as flexing at the poll will constrict the incoming air-flow and therefore make breathing uncomfortable. The horse's agility over fences will also be

restricted as its head and neck provides its balancing pole over hazards and fences.

The size and shape of the jaw must allow a bit to be fitted comfortably. Avoid a parrot mouth (where the top teeth jut out over the bottom teeth) as this precludes satisfactory bitting especially as regards a double bridle. For trouble-free bitting, the teeth of the upper and lower jaw should meet. Teeth should be regularly checked and rasped if necessary to avoid bitting problems.

Soundness

When buying any type of competition horse it is vital that it is thoroughly vetted by a specialist horse vet. An experienced veterinary surgeon can point out any potential pitfalls and offer advice as to whether or not they are potentially dangerous. It is up to the individual purchaser to decide whether they wish to have the horse's joints and feet X-rayed and its larynx endoscoped. Of course, even the most thorough vetting cannot guarantee a sound horse for ever more, but it can reduce the risk of spending a lot of money on the wrong horse. No horse is perfect, however, and just as a building surveyor can make a desirable property sound a dead loss, so a veterinary report can paint a bleak picture. In the end, the purchaser must decide which risks are acceptable and which are not. Surveyors and vets are not in the business of telling purchasers where to invest their money. They merely point out the pluses and minuses and the decision will always be the responsibility of the buyer.

Temperament

The horse's temperament depends on its willingness to please and its enthusiasm to carry out its work. As I mentioned earlier, a horse that finds its work easy will be easier to train.

The reverse can be experienced when the horse is forced to do things that it is too stiff and awkward to perform or does not understand. It takes time to build muscles and the pain caused by a bad back or aching tendons can make a genuine horse nervous and tense or even bad tempered and angry. Mental confusion may also lead to problems, for example whether to jump over or into water. It must be remembered that horses' backs were not designed to carry humans over large fences. Bad riding and badly fitting saddles do not always make it easy for the horse to remain co-operative! Attention must always be paid to detail when fitting saddlery and it is equally important to show consideration in the way we sit on the horse.

Vetting a horse for purchase

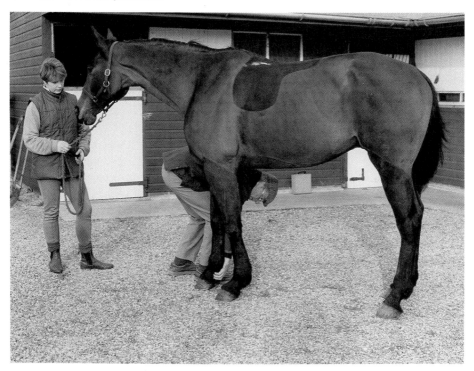

Natural Ability

Natural ability speaks for itself but I think attitude and courage could also be included in this section. The horse must have a natural aptitude for the sport. In Germany there is a very well-organised breeding programme to ensure that horses wanted for dressage are bred from one certain line and jumpers from another. Theoretically, this means that the horse should have an inherited aptitude for the job it is expected to do. In Great Britain the notion of the importance of correct breeding for competition is growing but, naturally, a breeding programme takes years to develop. There have always been popular stallions for breeding eventers but until now not enough emphasis has been put on the mares' ability.

Courage is an essential quality but one that is difficult to assess until training has begun. Some horses have lovely conformation but lack the required competitive drive and so prove very disappointing. Others, that have a good mental attitude, can thus overcome some of their physical defects so long as they do not cause unsoundness.

Type

First of all, you must decide at which level you wish to compete. The higher up the scale you go, the nearer to the Thoroughbred you must go, although a degree of common blood is always desirable as the true Thoroughbred tends to be more susceptible to minor knocks and bruises than its coarser-bred cousins. An ideal breeding is probably seven-eights or threequarters

Thoroughbred. The reason for this is that as the speeds get faster, the more difficult it becomes for a more common-bred horse to make the time. I once rode a very courageous half-bred mare who competed up to Advanced level but she had to go flat out from start to finish and she still had time faults!

Overall, the look of the horse should suggest power, athleticism and honesty. Just as beauty is said to be in the eye of the beholder, so is perfection! When you see a horse for the first time you will get a feel of whether it is the right one for you. First impressions are vital and you must like what you see. If you don't, then don't buy it.

THE RIDER

Experience for eventing is obtained through the normal development of enjoying riding. Basic lessons that improve position and balance will help you to gain a secure, independent seat at walk, trot and canter. Jumping lessons should run alongside your work on the flat, to build confidence.

My own youth was spent in many happy hours 'playing' with ponies. We had the most exciting time as cowboys and indians, which was an ideal way to improve balance (most of the time we rode without saddles), control of our ponies and our ability to get across country, all of which helped to develop confidence. I realise that such opportunities are not so available nowadays when there is less open country in which to ride, farming has become intensive and ponies more expensive, but although it is important to have formal lessons it is equally important to have fun and learn to do things naturally.

Hunting and drag-hunting offer a means of gaining experience across country, although the jumping with some packs is minimal these days. With all packs, hunting is expensive and there is always a high risk of injury to the horse.

The most-important qualities in an event rider are:
U patience
U stamina and dedication
U hardwork
U confidence
U courage

Before entering your first event, go to as many unaffiliated (not registered) dressage and show jumping competitions as possible. These are held throughout the twelve months of the year, both indoors and out of doors. Hunter trials are usually held during the spring and autumn and offer experience of riding over natural obstacles and terrain. It is important that the rider can remain in balance when jumping up and down slopes as well as over fences on the flat.

When you at last decide to begin competing, start with a novice, unaffiliated event at the local Pony Club (if a junior) or the local Riding Club if you are an adult. If you have

Competitor going cross-country in a Pre-Novice

competed happily in your youth and wish to continue with BHS horse trials, find a suitable Pre-Novice as a first experience. If you are unfamiliar with the standard of severity of your local courses, *Eventing* magazine gives a very good assessment of all the events.

EQUIPMENT

Having all the equipment that is available would be nice but it is not essential. At the end of the day, it is just you and your horse who have to complete the course and no amount of expensive transport, rugs and other accessories are going to improve your performance. Do not be intimidated by large sponsored event teams, as being a member of one of them has its own drawbacks. To compete at Intermediate and Advanced levels is an entirely different ball game in terms of finance and time commitment and here being sponsored is often the only answer.

No matter what your pocket allows, the turnout of both horse and rider must always be tidy. First impressions are important and are something you never have a second chance to improve on. It is therefore vital that your horse is properly groomed, plaited and presented. For the dressage, the horse will need a snaffle bridle and a saddle. A general purpose saddle, which is suitable for all disciplines, is a basic necessity. A straighter-cut saddle for dressage is useful but not essential. A forward-cut saddle for the cross-country is vital to enable the rider to get forward over the horse's centre of balance.

For the Rider

The rider must wear hunting dress, which means either a blue, black or tweed jacket with beige breeches and a tie or stock, or a uniform. It is essential that your boots are very clean and highly polished. Even rubber boots can support a shine good enough 'to see your face in' with the help of ordinary furniture polish. Anytime when you are mounted, the rules require you to wear a hard hat. Ladies must keep their hair tidy in a hairnet and any gloves worn must be of a light colour.

The same dress is worn for the show jumping phase, except that the hard hat must now be either British Standard BSI 6473 or a crash helmet, which provides more protection and bears the British Standard number BSI 4472. Over the crash helmet you must wear a dark silk.

For the Horse

The equipment for the horse can be changed for the jumping phases if required. Some horses require a different bit for each of the different phases, others remain in a snaffle throughout. The important thing is that the rider remains in control!

A breastplate and surcingle are advisable and can have a martingale attached if necessary. The holding straps on the girth will prevent the surcingle from sliding back. Rawhide or buffalo hide leathers and stainless steel irons are also advisable, as they do not break.

If leather reins are used for the dressage, they should be replaced with either rubber-covered or continental webbing reins to prevent your hands from slipping, especially

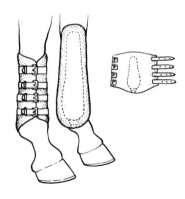

brushing boot

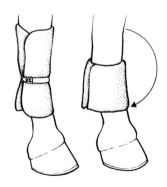

Yorkshire boots

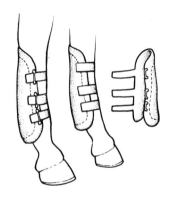

tendon boot

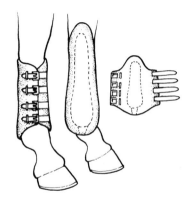

a speedicut boot

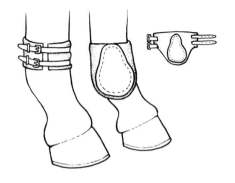

fetlock boots

sausage boots

Different types of boots

on the cross-country. It is also advisable to use a bootlace or some strong plaiting thread to secure the headpiece of the bridle to a plait just behind the horse's ear, in case you come off.

Boots or bandages are a wise precaution to protect the horse's legs. If boots are used they must be strong enough to be effective but supple enough to prevent any sores. Bandages must always be carefully applied so that the tension is even. They should also have gamgee or something similar fitted underneath them. Finally, they should be secured with either strong sewing thread or adhesive tape, to prevent them from coming undone, again being careful to keep the tension the same as that of the bandage. Vetwrap bandages are expensive but very effective. They are sticky on both sides and so can be

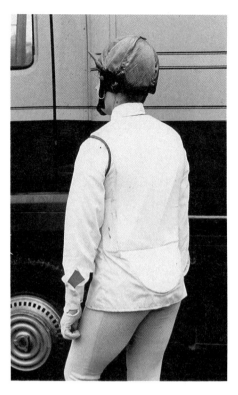

Back protector

securely fitted without constricting the flow of blood. Over-reach boots should also be worn to protect the heels of the front feet. It is a sensible idea to work your horse each day in ordinary brushing boots to prevent any unnecessary injury. Over-reach boots need only be added when you are jump schooling or galloping. Their occasional use during training will accustom the horse to the feel of these additional accoutrements.

The rider will wear the same equipment for the cross-country as for the show jumping, except for changing their jacket for a jumper and the dark silk on their skull cap for a brightly coloured one. You must always wear a back protector. There are now several different types on the

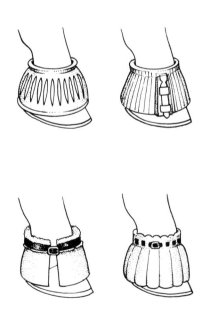

Over-reach boots

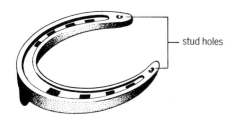

Front shoe showing the site of the stud holes

market, which offer padded protection for all over the upper body in the case of a fall. Each competitor is also expected to provide their own number bib and medical card holder when competing at any BHS horse trials. These can be obtained from the Horse Trials office at Stoneleigh.

For the jumping phases, and in some cases for the dressage as well, it may be necessary to fit studs into the

Mordax road stud

Square jumping stud

Pointed jumping stud

shoes of the horse. Normally, the shoes are made of fullered, concave, light iron with the stud holes inserted in the heel of the shoe about 1 cm (½ in) from the end. I believe it is necessary to have one on each side of the shoe so that the balance of the foot is maintained. Some horses will also require studs in their front shoes, as any form of slipping will cause them to lose confidence. Studs in the front shoes can shorten the horse's action and, in some cases, can also cause unlevel steps but slippery conditions are just as likely to inhibit the stride and sap the confidence of the horse. The type of stud used will depend upon the weather and the condition of the going but as a general guide the thin sharp ones are best for the front shoes, with the square variety in the hind shoes.

Another controversial subject is the use of cushion pads when the going becomes hard during the summer months. These are fitted under the front shoes to reduce concussion. There are many types on the market and the best person to consult about these is your farrier as he will be up to date with the latest ideas on the subject. I have not had a lot of success with the more expensive ones but have found a thick leather pad under the front shoes quite helpful. A wide web shoe will spread the concussion as well as protecting the sole if the feet are a little flat.

Facilities

The use of good facilities is essential for the thorough training of your horse but it is not vital to have your own as nowadays schooling arenas and cross-country fences are available for hire in all parts of the country.

If you intend to event seriously, it will be important to have your horse stabled. This problem is also surmountable as there are numerous livery yards and do-it-yourself yards that are willing to hire out individual stables and, in many cases, facilities as well, in a bumper bundle. There are also many natural training opportunities that can be used while exercising your horse, such as teaching the horse to trot and canter up and down hill, paddle through water, hop over a ditch or log and many other natural hazards. The important thing is to remain observant and take advantage of any opportunties that become available.

Transport

Some form of transport is essential if any amount of eventing is to be done. Hiring transport is possible but very expensive. There are firms that hire a lorry complete with a driver and others who hire a lorry or trailer for you to drive yourself. Either way, the only feasible thing to do is to try to share the cost with someone else, otherwise it becomes completely prohibitive. There are strict regulations regarding vehicles used for transport and cars that pull trailers in order to protect horses' welfare. Before purchasing any vehicle intended for this purpose, it is advisable to seek professional advice to ensure that its weight-carrying capacity conforms with current regulations. Your local Department of Transport will have knowledge of all current regulations. All lorries have to be plated annually, which is a

similar test to the MOT for a car. If the lorry is over a certain weight, the driver must pass a heavy goods vehicle driving test before being allowed to drive it on public roads.

Horseboxes All types of horseboxes are expensive but they offer the safest and most comfortable form of transport for the horse. They can vary in quality from the very basic to the very luxurious. The most basic of all is a cattle lorry, which lacks padding and insulation and can be draughty and noisy. A custom-built lorry will offer more comfort but the ventilation arrangements must always be checked. Several of the smart, new lorries on the market do not allow enough fresh air to circulate and the atmosphere quickly becomes stuffy. Sliding windows made of toughened glass and adjustable vents or roof ventilators will ensure plenty of fresh air without draughts. Modern aluminium or glassonite lorries are both lighter in weight than the old-fashioned kind and require less maintenance than a wooden box.

The floor and ramp must be safe and non-slippery. Rubber or rubber grannalistic matting is the most satisfactory covering for the floor and ramp, although it is also the most expensive. If the ramp is left as plain wood it must have gripper treads and then a covering of either straw or shavings. It is important to have lightweight gates at the top of the ramp, to assist with loading as well as to ensure that the horse does not try to step down as the ramp is lowered.

Horses appear to travel best facing

Right: **Two different types of lorry**

forwards, backwards or herringbone, i.e. diagonally across the lorry. It is advisable to have an easily moved partition between each horse so that they cannot tread on each other. I prefer the bottom part of the partition to have a rubber skirt so that the horse can spread its legs comfortably. If horses feel restricted and cannot maintain their balance, they soon become awkward to load and troublesome to travel.

Trailers The alternative type of transport is a trailer. These vary considerably in size and weight and are best towed by a four-wheel drive vehicle. It is vital that the towing bar is at the correct height so that the trailer travels level. The trailer has a joint lighting system with the towing vehicle and this must be checked before loading the horse. The latest models also have an automatic braking system which prevents the trailer from breaking away from the vehicle but it is a good idea to have an extra-strong safety chain as well, just to guard against all eventualities.

The two-horse trailer is the most popular. These come in two types:
1. front and rear ramp
2. single rear ramp only
The front-unload type is obviously

Trailer showing front unload

more expensive but it is the safer version. Horses are less likely to rush out forwards than backwards, so the risk of injury is less. If the front ramp is lowered before loading, this will encourage a less confident horse to go in as it can see the way out. Whenever you load, always fasten the breeching strap behind the horse to prevent it from rushing out backwards. There should always be a breast bar fitted in front of the horse to give it support while travelling. Whenever the trailer is parked and the occupants are left inside, for example at a show, the legs at each corner of the trailer should be let down to provide extra stability. Always remember to raise them again before moving off! A jockey wheel, fitted to the towbar of the trailer, is a worthwhile extra for help in hitching up and if the trailer has to be moved without a towing vehicle. A side, groom's door is also essential, in both a lorry and a trailer, in case the horses need attention during their journey.

The larger trailers, intended for three or four horses, are very heavy and cumbersome to handle and the ability to brake could be debatable. The single-horse trailer is small and cramped for its passenger, and tends to be top heavy, making it difficult to corner. It is also very susceptible to cross winds.

Anyone unfamiliar with driving a lorry or trailer should practise with an empty vehicle. It is important to avoid any sudden braking or acceleration and taking corners too fast. It is also unwise, and in some cases dangerous, to drive too fast. It is best not to exceed 60 kmph (40 mph) even on the best roads.

When travelling to an event you must take a responsible person with you, who can drive and double-up as a groom. It is totally irresponsible to expect the horse trials secretary to cope with your horse, lorry (and very often dog) if you have a fall and are unable to look after them yourself. It is also sensible to write your name, address and telephone number, together with the name of your next of kin, on a piece of paper stuck inside your hat and number cloth. In the event of an accident, this saves valuable time. Even if the dreaded accident never occurs, it is advantageous to have a co-driver if you are tired and a willing ear to listen to all the 'if onlys' on the long journey home. Alternatively, if you have won the championship it is wonderful to join in the celebrations, knowing that your driver will get you home safely!

SUMMARY

1. An event horse must have the conformation to enable it to do its job easily and remain sound. It must have a good temperament, some natural ability and be of the type that can gallop without effort.
2. The rider must have patience, stamina, confidence, courage and the ability to work hard.
3. The rider must have developed a secure, independent seat and have experience of riding over all types of terrain.
4. Essential equipment required by the horse:
   i) Appropriate bridle and saddle.
   ii) Breastplate – with martingale

attachment if required – and surcingle.

iii) Boots or bandages to protect the legs of the horse and over-reach boots to protect the heels of the front feet.

iv) Rubber-covered or continental web reins for the cross-country, to prevent the hands slipping.

v) Studs, if the going is wet and slippery or excessively dry.

5. Essential equipment for the rider:

i) Jacket, beige breeches, boots, light-coloured gloves, stock or tie, hairnet and a hard hat BSI number 6473 or the BSI 4472 which is compulsory for the cross-country phase.

ii) A dark silk for the dressage and show jumping and a coloured silk for the cross-country to complement the cross-country jumper or top.

6. The use of good facilities is essential for the training of your horse but it is not vital to own them as they can be hired.

7. Some form of transport becomes essential if you are to start eventing seriously.

8. There are two different forms of transport, i.e. a horsebox or a trailer.

9. A Body protector will offer valuable protection in the case of a fall.

CHAPTER FOUR

PREPARING FOR A ONE-DAY EVENT

Success in anything is achieved by correct training and paying attention to detail. Fitness is the first requirement of any horse that is going to event. Three months should be allowed to get it from soft grass condition to ready for a BHS Novice event. Gradual preparation will ensure that it stays fitter and, with luck, sounder, longer.

Before starting any training programme, the basic principles of good stable management must be covered. The horse must be wormed when it is first brought in and the process repeated every six weeks thereafter. The worming schedule should be planned in advance so that it does not clash with any of your competitions. Flu and tetanus vaccinations must be brought up to date with current competition rules and an entry made by your veterinary surgeon to this effect on the horse's passport. If these vaccinations are done during the walking stage of fittening, they will not interrupt the serious work later on. The horse's teeth should also be checked and rasped if necessary and continue to be looked at by the equine dentist every six months; some horses will need attention at more frequent intervals. Finally, before work starts shoes must be fitted.

I always make myself a chart of the fittening programme and pin it up in the tack room. It gives details of the work that is to be done by the horse each day, specifying hacking, fast work, dressage and jump schooling. Another chart shows diet, worming, vaccinations and the shoeing programme. These charts are used as a guideline to monitor the horse's progress and can be altered to suit each individual horse but this method does mean that the work is definitely supervised and facilities can be booked ahead when you need them.

Two types of fittening programme are used by competitors. The first is the traditional method and the other is interval training. Both will get the horse fit if carried out properly, but I feel the traditional method is the safest one to use if you are training on your own and/or are inexperienced. It will be quite adequate for a one-day event. If you aspire to the higher flights of three-day horse trials, more dedicated and specific training practices will be called for.

TRADITIONAL FITTENING

Weeks	Start by walking for
1–4	threequarters of an hour, gradually working up to one and a half hours to two

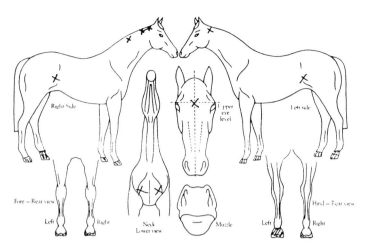

Name of animal **BIZARRE BIZARRE.** No.

Colour **APPALOOSIAN.** Sex **MARE** Date of Birth **1978.** Approx. Adult Height **16H2**

Head **MEDIUM HAIR WHORL ON UPPER EYE LEVEL.**

Neck **HAIR WHORLS RIGHT & LEFT CREST.**

LEGS
LF **STRIPED HOOF.**
RF **STRIPED HOOF.**
LH **WHITE TO HALF CORONET. STRIPED HOOF.**
RH **STRIPED HOOF.**

Body **HAIR WHORLS RIGHT AND LEFT FLANKS. HAIR WHORL. LEFT ANTERIOR DORSAL CREST. HAIR WHORL. RIGHT POSTERIOR DORSAL CREST. DOUBLE FEATHERED HAIR WHORL RIGHT ANTERIOR DORSAL CREST.**

Place and Date **STUD FARM MOULTON. 15.3.90.**

V.S. Stamp and signature
A.S.M. GORDON
B.V.M.S. M.R.C.V.S.

Identification procedure: The above identification must be completed by a Veterinary Surgeon only.

The recommended procedure for identification is described in the F.E.I. booklet 'Identification of Horses'.

The diagram and written description must agree and must be sufficiently detailed to ensure the positive identification of the animal in future. White markings must be shown in red and the written description completed using **black ink in black capitals or typescript.** If there are no markings, this fact must be stated in the written description.

All head and neck whorls should be marked ("X") and described in detail. Other whorls should be similarly recorded in greys and in animals lacking sufficient other distinguishing marks. Acquired marks ("——") and other distinguishing marks, e.g. prophet's thumb mark ("∧"), will, except, etc., should also be noted.

Age: In the absence of documentary evidence of age, animals older than 8 years may be described as "aged".

Please leave blank: 'signalment key' top right hand box and 'No'.

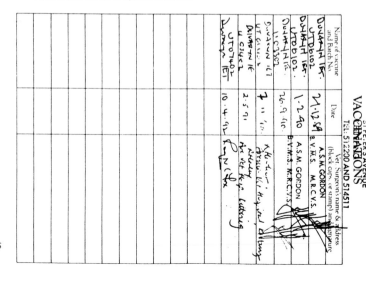

hours by week four. Start trotting for short periods during the second week and increasing the length of the trot as the horse develops. If the horse has enjoyed the traditional summer at grass and has put on excessive fat, the period of walk will need to be extended to rid it of this obesity. If you have some little hills nearby, introduce some hillwork. Never make the horse blow or sweat excessively at this stage.

Weeks 5–8 Keep the length of work at two hours per day. Start some dressage schooling and jumping training. Introduce short periods of canter. Gradually increase the effort required so that the heart works harder, thus increasing the stamina Gentle hillwork is ideal for this purpose. In the absence of any hills, the work must just be increased. Towards the middle of this period, it should be possible to include going to some small dressage and show jumping competitions.

Weeks 9–12 The canter work now needs to be done twice weekly. At first the canter is carried out at a speed of 24 kmph (15 mph) working up to twelve minutes' duration. As the event draws closer, the distance must be shortened and the speed made faster. Again, if hills can be used this will increase the work load without increasing the speed, which will help to preserve the horse's legs. During the last couple of weeks the horse can compete in hunter trials to replace the canter work. This will help to improve its jumping and acclimatise it to the world of competition again.

INTERVAL TRAINING

This follows the same pattern as the traditional method for the first six weeks as the horse requires to be at a stage of basic fitness before it starts the canter work. This method puts limited stress on the horse followed by a period of semi-rest before asking the horse to repeat the work again. As the horse progresses, there is an increase in the number of periods of canter and more effort and speed are asked for. Throughout the work, careful monitoring and recording of the horse's heart rate, respiration and recovery rate must be carried out. To do this properly, a second, dismounted person is required so that the necessary records can be made. It is not always possible to have that important help readily available.

The rider must also make an effort to be properly fit so that they are capable of helping the horse to the end of the cross-country. I have often seen overweight riders flopping about and hindering the horse towards the end of the course. If you are preparing your own horse for a one-day event,

Horse in fit eventing condition

you will probably gain a certain amount of fitness from riding every day. Being a little asthmatic myself, I have found it beneficial in the past to run a short distance each day to ensure that I will be able to breathe properly on the way round. I now have an exercise bike which I set up in front of a good television programme and that has the same effect! Some riders find that it helps to sing as they exercise their horses, as this encourages more energetic breathing and the benefits which that provides, apart from the interest and applause that it may attract from bystanders. To increase physical fitness, at least one of our leading event riders used to ride a bicycle with the saddle removed over long distances. To sit down would have been remarkably uncomfortable but the effort paid off in the end.

TRAINING

The aim of training any horse is to have it well balanced, supple and with a good mouth so that it will be obedient to the rider's aids. With obedience comes trust and respect from both sides, as this situation cannot be reached when horse and rider are in conflict with each other. As with children, the happiest horse is the one who has some discipline and knows some boundaries. Too much discipline can lead to rebellion later on, however, so a happy medium must be reached whereby respect is achieved without fear.

The basic training of the young horse can be split into different sections. There is no set point when progress to the next step must be taken, as this is different with each individual. What is important is that each lesson is firmly established and

A horse working long and low to loosen its muscles before work begins

41

its objectives attained before moving on. It is also vital that a logical sequence is followed so that if a problem is experienced the horse can be taken back to a previous stage before being asked to progress again.

Each schooling session should begin with loosening up the muscles. This should not take too long because then the horse will start to use up the energy it will require to perform its work. Each horse requires a different amount of time to warm up so it is important that you get to know how much your own particular horse requires. Bearing in mind that horses respond very well to routine, we can turn this to our advantage in the training. Always carry out the same method of warming up and period of concentration at home and at the event. My ideal warm-up period before a dressage test is about 45 minutes. If the horse is fresh at a competition I find that ten minutes on the lunge, where it can get rid of its exuberance and loosen its muscles, is far less exhausting for both of us, and then the proper work can be begun in a more relaxed frame of mind.

Training on the flat is vital, as most of the problems that are experienced over fences are usually an exaggeration of a problem experienced on the flat. The initial stages of schooling must try to achieve calmness and have the horse going freely forward in a rounded shape. Rhythms and straightness will develop as the horse progresses. The inside hindleg must be encouraged to work underneath the horse so that it can lower its croup and 'sit back', thus achieving self-carriage. The

rider's hand on the rein must be allowing and the horse's jaw relaxed. Most resistance in the mouth is caused by the horse not using its hindquarters and back correctly.

The Aids

Communication between the rider and the horse is referred to as the aids. These are the signals through which we indicate our wishes to the horse. They must be clear and precise so that no misunderstanding can arise. Our legs are our strongest asset and should be used before any hand aids. Transitions from one pace to another will help the horse to balance itself and use its hindlegs properly – if it fails to do this it will use its head and neck to balance, thus developing the underside of its neck.

The half-halt is another very useful movement, which can be used to rebalance the horse throughout its training. It is performed by the rider closing their legs around the horse and applying just enough restriction via the hand to slow the horse down. As it slows, the hand relaxes and 'allows', and the legs increase their pressure to push the horse forward. This improves the engagement of the hocks. The canter aid must always be very clear so that the horse does not become confused. Basic lateral work will also help the engagement of the horse's hindleg and thus improve its self-carriage.

Problems will arise during the training of any horse for either dressage or jumping and they must be corrected as soon as they occur. It is important for anyone who embarks on training to have an experienced person to help from the ground. Even

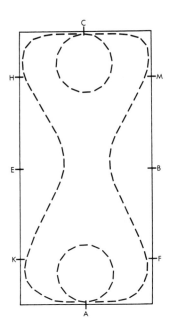

A good suppling exercise is a shallow loop with a small circle at each end of the arena

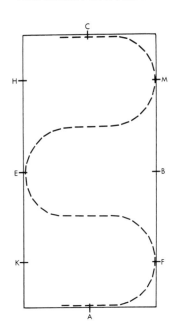

This can progress into a serpentine

our most experienced Olympic riders have a trainer, so it must follow that the less experienced will definitely benefit from the old saying 'two heads are better than one'! Various movements from dressage tests can be practised but it is unwise to practise them in the sequence of the test you are about to do at a competition as it does not take long for an intelligent horse to anticipate and begin 'jumping the gun'.

One movement that can be repeatedly practised, however, is the entry and halt. Work on this until it is perfect as it will get you off to a good start each time. One of the most difficult things to achieve is to ride a straight line and a square halt, especially on a very fit horse.

All movements must always be correctly ridden, showing round

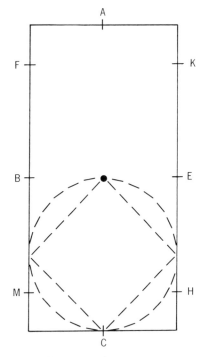

A circle ridden correctly

circles and serpentines of equal dimensions – the secret is to pay attention to detail. In the lengthened strides or medium paces, be careful not to hurry so that you push the horse off balance.

Jumping Training

It is even more important to have someone on the ground when you begin jumping schooling. There are several reasons for this. The first and most serious is the safety aspect. If you and/or your horse have a fall or sustain an injury while jumping, there will be someone on hand to help – even if this is only to catch a loose horse. From a practical point of view, it is always better to have someone to move poles and replace fences that have been knocked down, as well as to offer advice on how the performance can be improved.

From whatever pace the horse is asked to jump, the same principles that applied in the dressage will apply again. It must be able to maintain its balance and rhythm while going forward at all times. Correct training and experience over a variety of fences and terrain will produce confidence and make the horse a pleasure to ride.

Jumping will automatically improve your work on the flat by making the horse stretch its back and use itself. Many top dressage horses are jumped over small fences to loosen their back muscles, although admittedly not always ridden by their regular partners!

Calmness is all important while jumping because if the horse becomes tense it will be unable to use itself properly. Work over poles on the ground or slightly raised will

Work over poles on the ground will encourage the horse to use itself correctly

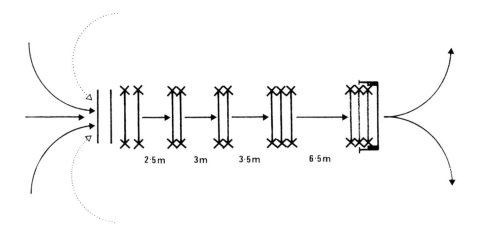

Gridwork can be very beneficial

encourage the horse to bends its joints. If the horse is accustomed to using poles, they can be used again if the horse needs to have the point of take-off adjusted nearer to a fence.

Gridwork is especially helpful to give the horse confidence in combination fences and to help supple it, make it more athletic in its performance and increase its ability to alter or adjust its stride on the approach to an obstacle. It is very important that the horse learns to be clever and agile so that it can get itself out of a tricky situation.

The approach to any fence must be straight and complete freedom should be given to the horse in the air, but a slight contact must be maintained to assist balance. You cannot practise the art of show jumping enough and all event horses should have various low-grade show jumping competitions included in their training programme. Many unaffiliated competitions are organised all over the country, as well as affiliated competitions for horses

that are registered with the BSJA. A horse that is expected to perform at a BHS Novice event should be quite happy to jump a Newcomers course. I have always tried to do as many show jumping competitions as possible before the start of the event season, for my own benefit as much as that of the horse.

Event riders are renowned for seeing long strides and asking for a huge stand off. This comes from riding in an attacking manner across country at speed but it can prove to be very expensive at an event if the horse has fences down just because of this. Practice will make perfect!

Cross-country Fences

The cross-country phase will pose a variety of different fences to be jumped over varying terrain. Some will require a bold, attacking approach while others will need a careful, bouncy approach.

Solid Sloping Fences As a general rule, if the fence is sloping away from

Jumping at local competitions will help to improve your show jumping technique

you and has a well-defined groundline, it can be attacked. Keep the horse balanced between your hand and leg aids and approach the fence with lots of impulsion. Such fences would include:

ʊ steeplechase fences
ʊ ascending parallels
ʊ triple bars
ʊ log piles
ʊ fences with a ditch on take-off

Any fence that incorporates a ditch must be approached positively to make the spread.

Upright fences These command caution and respect from the rider and must be approached with more care. If there is a filling in front of the upright, however, it becomes a lot more straightforward and can be approached with little change of speed. A truly upright fence such as a:

ʊ gate
ʊ post and rails
ʊ Helsinki rails
ʊ wall

all require a controlled approach and here it will be necessary to slow down and get the horse off its forehand to jump them successfully. Obviously, the slowing down must not take too long so that only the minimum amount of time is lost.

True parallels and table fences also require that the horse is organised on

Where to jump an upright

take-off in order to prevent a nasty moment or even a fall. They will need a little more impulsion in order to clear the spread.

Banks Never encourage your horse to bank a fence that can be jumped, such as a hayrack or table. Banks need to be approached in a similar way to the parallel – spend a few strides getting the horse onto its hocks and in a good balance and then ride forward positively.

Jumping from Light to Shade These fences must always be ridden strongly as the horse's natural instrict will be to distrust such an obstacle. It is also difficult to judge the take-off. Allowance must also be made for the eyes to adjust from light to dark once you have negotiated the obstacle. This is another time when you must be sure to have the horse off its forehand and between your hand and leg so that you can ride for a rounder type of jump.

Jumping Uphill Galloping uphill will free the horse's shoulder and its hindlegs will automatically come underneath it. Few problems are experienced in jumping uphill as long as the impulsion is maintained. You must start to ride forward strongly about four or five strides away from the fence to ensure that there is sufficient petrol in the tank!

Jumping Downhill Galloping downhill is always difficult and jumping downhill can be very dangerous if the horse is allowed to fall onto its forehand, lean on the rider's hands and lengthen its stride. Once this happens the hocks fall out behind it and all the jumping power is lost. These fences must always be jumped carefully and slowly. On an inexperienced horse, it may even be necessary to trot down a steep slope before a fence to ensure a trouble-free passage. At this type of fence safety must come before speed.

Steps

Steps Steps or a series of banks must always be approached with a lot of impulsion. The same would apply if there was a bank to jump up with a fence directly after it or if there was a ditch in front of the first element. The secret is for the rider to approach the obstacle with confidence and lots of impulsion.

Drop Fences Jumping off a bank should not cause any problems as it should only feel like landing over a fence. The rider should remain forward so as not to put any weight on the weak part of the horse's back. The approach to all drop fences must be positive and confident. As my father used to say to my sister and me, 'Horses have very adequate brakes on their own when they see a drop!' The contact on the rein must be maintained through a following

hand, while still allowing the horse to stretch its head and neck.

Combinations Combinations come in a variety of different types and distances:

ᘮ sunken road
ᘮ off-set rails
ᘮ coffin
ᘮ bank and rails
ᘮ rails and bank

Any type of fence that has another part at a set distance and is numbered together with the first element constitutes a combination. They all need careful planning and organisation of the horse by the rider on the approach. They are extremely difficult to ride on a tearaway horse that tends to jump itself into trouble, but can be equally difficult on a reluctant horse that runs out of impetus. The horse must be moving

Jumping off a bank, being careful not to put too much weight on to the weak part of the horse's back

freely forward but be attentive to the rider so that it can be pushed on or brought back as necessary. Any combination must be approached with lots of impulsion but do not confuse this with speed. During training, jump as many different types of combination as possible to develop trust and confidence between horse and rider. The fences do not need to be very big for this purpose as overfacing or a bad experience will do more harm than good to the horse.

Practice over combinations will help the horse to become more agile and encourage it to find an extra leg when necessary.

A sunken road must be approached slowly with a lot of impulsion so that you have enough spare petrol to drive on out of the obstacle. A coffin must also be approached in a similar manner, especially if it is on a downhill slope. The rider's legs must be driving forward quite strongly so that the horse cannot stop when it

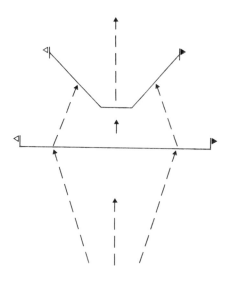

The route through a combination must be decided on before starting the course

course, pick out a landmark and ride a straight line across the corner to that point. Never look down, not even briefly, as you will lose direction and the horse may run out. Always remember that you go where you look, so look forward and ride forward. You must have perfect control in the approach, with the horse between hand and leg. Providing that the horse is used to jumping fences on an angle, corners should present few problems. This type of technical fence can also be practised at home during jump training sessions. This will help with the horse's education as well as giving the rider practice in presenting the horse on the correct line of approach.

sees the ditch, but the rider's hands must convert the power generated by the legs into energy rather than speed.

The route through a line of off-set rails must be decided upon before riding the course and firmly adhered to. Any last minute change of mind will spell disaster.

Bounce A bounce fence requires a very organised approach. It calls for a lot of controlled impulsion and a quick reaction from the horse. The distance between the two elements must be carefully measured when you walk the course so that it is ridden with sufficient confidence and does not tempt the horse to put in a small stride in the middle. Low bounce fences, made out of show jump poles can be practised at home during your gymnastic jump training.

Corner Fences When walking the

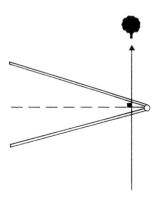

Pick out a landmark and ride a straight line across the corner to that point

Water and Ditches It is very important that the horse is never frightened by either of these obstacles. Its initial introduction to them is therefore of vital importance. Puddles at the side of the road and in fields offer an easy way to start the horse's water education. Small ditches, through which the horse can

Jumping a plain ditch

happily walk, provided they have a sound bottom, or over which it can trot, are an ideal way of building confidence. When riding over a ditch in a competition, most horses will normally have a brief moment of hesitation just before take-off. Approach the ditch in a good, balanced gallop and drop into the saddle and ride strongly forward during the last few strides. Ditches that form part of a combination fence have already been discussed.

It is natural for horses to fear water so every opportunity must be taken to allow the horse to go into water and play. Allow it to splash around, drink and get used to water being an enjoyable experience rather than something frightening. The water

should not be deep and the ground beneath it must have a firm base. While training the horse to jump into and out of water, it must be remembered that there are occasions, especially in the show jumping phase, when the horse will be asked to jump *over* water. Many an event horse has met its Waterloo by landing straight in the water in the show jumping phase instead of clearing it.

In competition, always reduce the speed going into water. If it is just a water splash, approach in trot but remember to keep a lot of impulsion and the horse going forward. Jumping an obstacle into water is about the most difficult of all types of fence. Never approach the fence with speed – depending on the size of the fence,

Adopt a secure seat when jumping into water

come in in either an active trot or a short, bouncy canter. Do not ask the horse to jump in big. The rider needs to sit up and keep their hands up with a good rein contact and with the seat and legs driving strongly forward. The landing from the jump is very often the crucial moment. This is about the only time I would definitely recommend the old-fashioned jumping seat, where the rider sits back and has the lower leg stuck forward. The rein contact must be kept firm so that the horse can use it to help rebalance itself; it will also enable the rider to keep the horse's head up. On landing, the horse should be encouraged to stay in trot as this will aid its stability. The canter stride causes more resistance from the water and subsequent loss of balance to the horse.

Alternative Fences When walking a cross-country course, the rider has to decide whether to take one route or another. The course builder will have designed both a quick way through, which will involve some form of risk of accumulating penalties, and a longer, safer but time-wasting route. It is up to the rider to decide whether the risk is feasible or not for their particular horse. Obviously, a novice or inexperienced horse is better to take the longer, safer route to ensure maintaining its rhythm and impulsion, while the more experienced horse may be able to take the quicker route to prevent incurring time penalties. Things that must be taken into consideration when deciding which way to go are:

- the capability of the horse
- the state of the going
- at what stage of the course it occurs
- the amount of time saved – especially if a period of collection is necessary

The thing always to remember is that it is better to lose a few seconds in time than risk a refusal, a fall or elimination.

Show Jumping

The show jumping phase does not ask as many questions of the horse as the cross-country but it can cause unnecessary faults just the same. Again, the important things to remember are to keep the horse in a good bouncy canter, maintain a rhythm and concentrate on the route taken. In its training at home the horse should have had practice over upright fences and parallel bars, with and without brightly coloured fillers. Going to lots of local shows will obviously help both horse and rider to gain valuable experience in jumping courses.

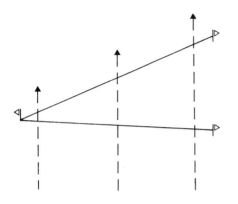

Alternative ways of jumping a fence

Judging Speed

The judgement of speed only comes with practice. Always do your canter work at home against a stop watch, which will help you to judge your speed and read the watch while travelling. Use an easy-to-read digital stop-watch and have an idea in your mind of where the halfway and threequarter markers are. Work out at what time you need to be at these places to be within the timescale allowed. Divide the course into fast and slow sections, giving yourself extra time in the slower parts. Beware of any parts that go through trees or long grass – you feel as though you are going a hundred miles an hour as the trees whiz by, only to find you have clocked up enormous time penalties when you return! Always remember to put safety first:

- ∪ keep the horse well balanced and in a good rhythm
- ∪ keep it going forward between hand and leg
- ∪ take the most feasible direct route
- ∪ do not allow the horse to gallop in a long flat shape, on its forehand and out of balance

Remember: balance and rhythm = safety!

A horse with a good bascule over the fence

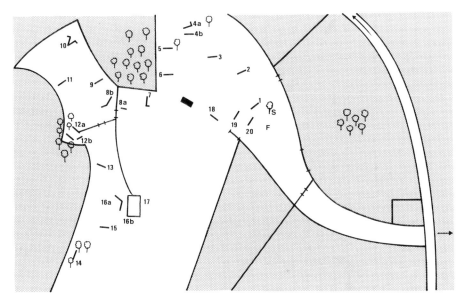

Plan of a cross-country course

As in the cross-country, an ascending parallel or triple bar can always be ridden stronger than an upright of planks or a gate. For the vertical fences and true parallels, you must have the horse well collected and back on its hocks so that it can lift its forehand over without hitting the fence. If the horse is allowed to become long and flat in its stride, it will not bascule, will hit the poles and collect unnecessary penalty points, spoiling the success you achieved in the other phases. Also, a horse that is allowed to become long and unbalanced is more likely to refuse than one that is kept short and bouncy with its hocks underneath it. A parallel fence off a corner is one type of fence that must be approached positively and with lots of impulsion. Another problem is when an upright fence is sited after a sloping spread on a related stride. This encourages the horse to become very long and flat.

WALKING COURSES

With both show jumping and cross-country courses, the golden rule is always to allow plenty of time for walking. If permitted, it is advisable to walk the cross-country course on the day before the competition, although this is unlikely to be possible for the show jumping course. You will be in a far more relaxed frame of mind and there will also be time for a second walk round if necessary. Try to go either on your own or with just one experienced friend or trainer, otherwise you cannot fully concentrate on the fences. Discourage chatty friends and fellow competitors. The former probably do not understand your need to concentrate; the latter may well have ulterior motives!

Always seek advice from an expert about difficult obstacles as this can often help you make your final decision. That final decision must always be yours, however, and once you have made it do not be persuaded to go a different way unless such things as climatic conditions make an alternative route more favourable. Indecision at any fence, but expecially at combination fences, is no decision at all and usually results in failure. Every single obstacle must be fully inspected and the distances between combinations properly measured. The pros and cons of alternative fences must be assessed so that once you have started you will know exactly where you are going and nothing will be left to chance. Certain landmarks need to be picked out so that straight lines can be ridden through tricky fences and the least amount of time can be taken in the safest way.

Terrain and current weather and ground conditions have to be taken into consideration. If the quickest route necessitates going through deep mud, it will probably be advisable to take a longer route and preserve the horse's energy.

When walking the show jumping course, the same basic rules apply. Walk the exact route you are going to ride. Study the individual fences, taking into account where the groundline is, what the filler is, how the fence before it may alter the way in which you need to jump the next one. With a tricky fence, make sure that there is nothing on the skyline that may confuse the horse's judgement of the height of the fence. For example, a distant building in sunlight may deceive the horse and make it look through the fence.

The position of the collecting ring and your horsebox should also be noted, especially when riding a novice or young horse. Horses are always attracted towards home and so a youngster may need to be ridden strongly away from home. Distances in combinations and fences that are close enough to be regarded as related fences must be carefully measured. If you are in doubt, watch a few horses jump round and see if the suspect distance is better ridden on three long strides or four short ones.

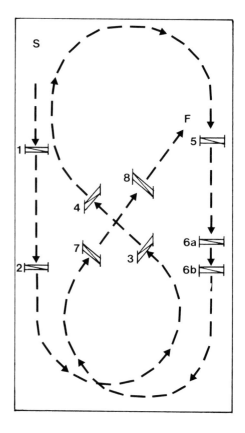

A plan of a show jumping course

SUMMARY

1. Success is achieved by correct training and paying attention to detail.
2. Fitness is vital for any horse and rider that are expected to event.
3. Dressage schooling must be included to teach the horse to balance itself and remain in rhythm. This is not done only so that good dressage marks can be achieved but also so that the horse will find the jumping easier.
4. Polework and grids will improve gymnastic ability and make the horse more athletic both on the flat and over fences.
5. A variety of different types of fence must be practised at home to build trust and confidence.
6. The horse must be between the rider's hands and leg aids at whatever speed it is travelling.
7. Certain fences require careful preparation of the horse on the approach.
8. Impulsion does *not* mean speed.
9. Always ride in good balance and with good rhythm to be safe.
10. Always allow plenty of time to walk the courses. If possible, try to walk the cross-country course the day before the event.
11. In each phase walk the exact track you want to ride. Inspect each fence carefully, measure the distances between obstacles and look at the going.

CHAPTER FIVE

OVERCOMING PROBLEMS

During the training of any animal there will be certain hiccups to overcome. The range of possibilities is far too vast to try to suggest cures for individual problems so I will simply explain the basic psychology of the horse so that its behaviour can be understood.

Under natural conditions, the horse is a nomadic creature. It is a trickle feeder, selecting the best grass and shrubs as it moves quietly from place to place. The first major change occurs when the horse is confined in a stable for long periods. It must receive sufficient exercise daily and, if possible, have a period out in the paddock in safe conditions. Common problems occurring from lack of work are the horse misbehaving and bucking. This is its natural instinct when it wants to remove anything unpleasant from its back. Restricted movement can also interfere with the

Horses are happiest in each others' company

Lack of work can cause problems such as bucking

horse's circulation, causing filling in the legs. Another stable management problem is boredom which causes horses to develop vices such as weaving.

The next unnatural situation we have put the horse in is its digestion of a completely different diet. The temperament of each horse must be fully understood so that the food we give it does not have an 'alcoholic' effect. This can cause problems such as being very excitable in the dressage and pulling hard over fences so that stronger bits may need to be tried.

In the wild horses live in herds with one leader and so are happiest in the company of other horses. If they are kept on their own they can become fretful and lose condition. If they have one constant companion

they can become inseparable and therefore impossible to compete with. It is therefore important to realise that all horses must be ridden firmly from the time they are broken so that they do not become nappy. It is perfectly natural for them to leave home at a slower pace than they return, as their stable becomes a substitute for the herd. Just be aware that when a clever course builder positions a corner fence near the horsebox park or has put a tricky fence facing away from the collecting ring, the horse may prefer to join its friends rather than continue on its own!

By nature the horse is very timid and uses its speed to run away from danger. By correct training, however, we can develop it into a bold,

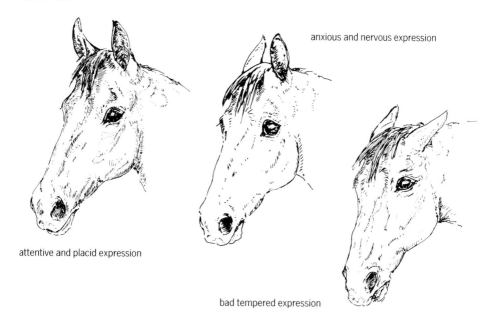

anxious and nervous expression

attentive and placid expression

bad tempered expression

The horse can express its feelings very easily

courageous creature. The horse has no reasoning power but does have an extremely long memory. For this reason, all training must be carried out in a logical sequence so that, should problems arise, you can return to an earlier stage. Throughout its schooling, a system of reward and punishment must be employed so that the horse knows what is expected of it. Basically, most horses are eager to please and so immediate praise or correction is vital. One of the problems most likely to occur from these natural instincts is rushing fences because the horse has remembered an unpleasant experience and is frightened. If punishment is incorrectly or excessively administered and the horse becomes frightened of its rider or trainer, its whole temperament can change and it can become headshy

or, worse still, nasty in the stable. This can work in the opposite way too, with the owner being too soft with the horse so that it becomes a typical spoilt child with no respect for anyone or anything. This type is equally unpleasant to work with and generally useless as a competitive horse. The best maxim is to praise lavishly and punish sparingly, never with gritted teeth, as this is likely to be caused by the rider's frustration rather than a deficiency in the horse's performance.

Horses also have acute senses of smell and hearing. These enable it to spot danger a long way away. For example, they have a natural fear of pigs, which can cause problems if your horse is kept on a farm with pigs or has to pass pigs on exercise. Their eyes are positioned on each side of their head, so they have a very wide field of vision. This can work against the horse giving a good dressage or jumping performance as it may shy at the boards around the arena or look back at something else when approaching a fence. Racehorses often wear blinkers or visors to keep them concentrating on what is happening in front of them but this is not allowed in either eventing or show jumping.

Because the horse was not designed as a weight-carrying creature, especially when being asked to jump over enormous obstacles that are both high and wide, we must remain aware of the danger we can cause to their backs and legs. Remember, if the horse is in pain its natural reaction will be to run away so if it works fast and hollow on the flat or over fences, have its back checked. If it suddenly starts to refuse to jump or will not strike off on a certain leg in canter, check its legs. If there is a lot of resistance in the mouth or an uncomfortably heavy feeling in the rein, have its teeth checked. Paying attention to detail is as important in stable management as it is when you are riding, and is the only way to success. If a problem occurs, have the horse checked by a veterinary surgeon to eliminate any physical problems. Then go to an experienced trainer who will surely help you.

If you begin to understand how the horse ticks and train it by encouraging what it considers to be a natural way of responding, success will be achieved much quicker. For example, when introducing a young or inexperienced horse to something new, take a more experienced companion along so that the youngster can follow. This uses the horse's natural desire to be with another horse to your advantage. Of course, there soon comes a time for the young one to go on its own, but it should have developed its own confidence by then.

Earlier, I briefly mentioned the benefit of using local competitions in preparation for the event season. These can usually be included in the last month of the fittening programme. In some cases it will be possible to do some dressage competitions earlier in your preparation period. These competitions are a superb training ground as your horse will probably lose concentration and may also react to any nerves you may be feeling and therefore produce a test that is much poorer in quality than you could achieve at home. It is important to iron out these minor hiccups and little dressage competitions will enable you and your horse to get into the swing of the competition circuit under less important circumstances. It is not only young horses that become excited at their first outing of the season, so the more experienced campaigner will also benefit from this type of outing. Near where I live there is an annual spring hunter trial which also runs some unaffiliated dressage. The whole world and his wife attend and any enthusiastic autograph hunter would have a field day! It offers a marvellous opportunity as it is the first chance of the year to do a dressage test out of doors followed by a cross-country course. The riders enjoy it because it heralds a new season and everyone catches up on the winter gossip (not

Local competitions provide an invaluable training ground

while walking the course, though!). The horses think it is wonderful to be outside after a winter indoors – and there are sometimes several empty saddles to prove it!

Even a horse that is not old enough or not yet ready actually to compete may well benefit from an outing involving travel, the excitement of other horses and people at the event, the noise of loud speakers and applause. The more used to these things the horse becomes the better it is when its turn comes to take part.

Jumping new and different cross-country courses will help to get your horse tuned up for a one-day event. Always inspect the hunter trial course carefully, as many of them are built by enthusiastic amateurs and are not officially inspected. Most of them are excellent and the basic standard is improving each year but do remember that it is better to miss out a fence than cause your horse to have a bad experience. Also, in the spring the ground conditions at hunter trials can be very deep if there has been a lot of rain. So, when you walk the course inspect the fences, the distances and the going carefully so that you and your horse will remain sound for your first one-day event.

Show jumping competitions will help you and your horse to get your eye in before the first important competition. If you can jump indoors during the winter, before the spring events begin, you will feel you have so much room when you come to

jump outside again! Also, if you have been jumping regularly, the fences will seem so much smaller at the first event, which is always an advantage.

These small affiliated or unaffiliated competitions are also essential for the rider. To be successful at anything you have to produce a certain amount of adrenalin but this must not cause tension which will upset the performance of your horse. Competing must always be fun otherwise there is no point in taking part but it is your duty to your horse not to let the occasion get the better of you so that you upset its performance. This is best achieved by taking part in lots of smaller competitions so that you both get used to such occasions and can take it all in your stride.

Hunter trials give an opportunity to practise cross-country fences

Practice Fences

The discipline in the practice area has been greatly improved now that the fences are flagged (red to be kept on your right and white to be kept on your left), this eliminating the risk of head-on collisions which used to be a quite frequent hazard. Also helpful is the rule that riders moving in opposite directions pass left hand to left hand. Nevertheless, there is still a chance of an accident through lax stewarding, other riders can cross your path in front of or behind the fence you are negotiating, or the horse jumping before you may dislodge a pole, interfering with your take-off or landing. Do not follow-my-leader too closely. Do not overjump the practice fence. Its purpose is to help horse and rider increase confidence, not to overexcite or exhaust either or both.

Do not treat your horse as a convenient, mobile grandstand. Whenever possible dismount and rest your horse's back, even at the expense of your own legs! It is far too common a sight at the smaller gymkhanas and shows to see riders eating ice-creams or chatting to their friends at the ringside while sitting on their horses.

SUMMARY

1. Understanding the natural instincts of the horse will help to explain some of the problems that may occur during training and competition.
2. It is invaluable for both the young horse and the experienced campaigner to compete in either affiliated or unaffiliated competitions to tune them up for a one-day event.
3. This also provides a good opportunity for the rider to become reaccustomed to the discipline and active participation of competition.
4. Discipline must be maintained in the practice area. No over-jumping. No use of horses as a grandstand.

Horse and rider trotting on the roads and tracks at a three-day event

This is my Horse
with his last owner.

Pony Club camp

Burghley House

Above: Horse and rider ready for the dressage phase

Left: Horse and rider ready for the cross-country phase

Above: Horse in grass condition

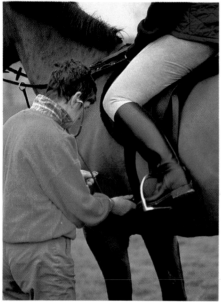

Left: Assistant taking the horse's pulse

Above: A sloping fence with a good
groundline will usually jump well

Right: Rider getting fit!

Jumping into shade

**Impulsion must be maintained while
jumping through a sunken road**

Gaining confidence in water

When a horse is turned out it
will revert to its natural life-style

Good manners must be observed in the practice ring at all times

Top right: Ideal competition yard

Bottom right: A hood on the horse will
help to keep the mane lying
flat when it is pulled short

A horse clipped in summer

The horse must be carefully inspected in the morning, evening and after work

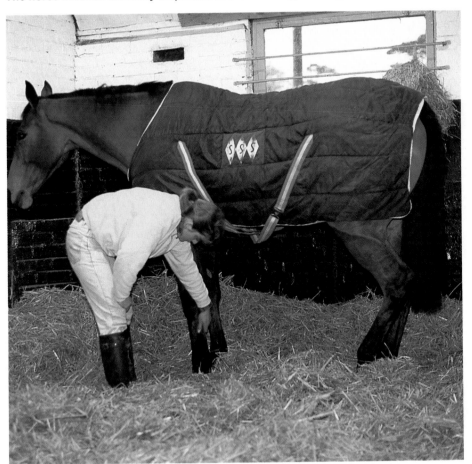

All finished for another day!

The next day – relaxing in the field!

CARE OF THE EVENT HORSE

THE STABLE

Every horse requires basic care in the stable, and this care is absolutely essential for the event horse. There are several basic rules which I will explain briefly as I cannot stress too many times the importance of paying attention to detail.

A stable of adequate size is a priority. The actual dimensions will vary according to the size of the horse. Wooden boxes are the cheapest to erect but tend to be hot in the summer and cold in the winter. This drawback can be largely overcome by good roof insulation.

The interior walls must be lined with boarding of sufficient strength to resist the effects of a horse kicking it. If the walls are unlined, not only is the insulation value reduced but a kick from the horse may remove the shiplap or weather boarding of the exterior wall as the force of the blow will be in the direction of the nails securing the boards. Despite the extra expense involved, interior lining should be provided to eaves level. Half-lined boxes are a false economy.

In my experience the very best type

Stable showing few fixtures

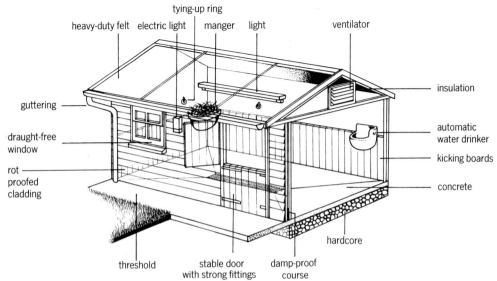

heavy-duty felt   electric light   tying-up ring   manger   light   ventilator

guttering

draught-free window

rot proofed cladding

threshold   stable door with strong fittings   damp-proof course   hardcore

insulation

automatic water drinker

kicking boards

concrete

of stable is built of stone as it remains very cool in the summer and can be warmer than my cottage in the winter! We do not always have the opportunity to choose our stable, but be aware of the advantages and disadvantages of each type. In the winter put plenty of rugs on the horse to keep it warm during cold weather.

A stable must be light and airy and contain as few fittings as possible. Feeding off the ground from a removable bowl will ensure that the horse eats in a natural way. Some horses tend to kick bowls over and lose the food, so they should be fed from a fixed manger. There are three methods of feeding hay: from haynets, hayracks or loose on the ground. Each method has its advantages and disadvantages. It is not within the scope of this book to discuss the merits or demerits of one method over another. Experience will enable you to make your choice. I would recommend that the hay is soaked before feeding as an increasing number of horses develop respiratory problems through the spores and dust found in hay. For the same reason, I would recommend that any horse that is expected to do fast work is bedded on either wood shavings or paper.

The stable must have adequate ventilation but no draughts. A Sheringham window, which has the top section opening inwards, will allow a fresh supply of air to circulate. Ridge ventilators are desirable to allow hot air to escape, especially during summer months. These ventilators need not be of the elaborate design of old traditional stabling and can be a comparatively simple outlet spaced along the ridge.

In extreme cold, the ridge ventilator can be blocked off. The window should be on the same side of the stable as the door so that there is no draught. It must be made of toughened glass and be protected by iron bars or steel mesh, which should accommodate the open position of the upper window. Spacing between the bars or mesh must not be wide enough to trap a foot should the horse become cast.

Any electrical fittings must be covered by some form of protection so that they cannot be broken. The light switch must be made of heavy insulated material and be positioned outside the door out of the reach of the horse.

An old-fashioned bucket is still considered to be the most satisfactory method of watering horses. Make sure that the horse has two full buckets at all times in the stable. A horse that is undergoing any form of rigorous training needs access to a lot of fresh, clean water, especially in warm weather. Horses have an ability to ration themselves as regards their supply of water. Do not be misled by the fact that the horse has not drunk all its bucket of water when you first open the stable in the morning. It may well be 'leaving something for later'. My experience is that if a late-night watering routine is adopted, the horse will drink more in the knowledge that the supply will be replenished.

For many horses the provision of automatic water bowls may be the answer. Of the various types available, the one with a float chamber with a simple ballcock operation is preferable to those operated by a lever depressed by the animal's nose. These are more suitable for cattle for which they were originally designed. Even so, some horses object to drinking from bowls and, of course, their intake of liquid cannot be monitored. In normal weather conditions and light work the average horse will consume between 36–45 litres (8–10 gal) of water per day. This will increase if the weather is hot and/or the horse undertakes strenuous work. It has been proved that water starvation is a prime cause of colic.

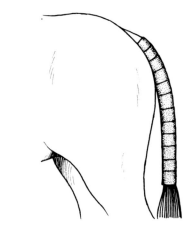

Tail bandage

GROOMING

A fit horse on a high concentrate diet secretes a considerable amount of waste product through its skin, so thorough grooming is essential. This also promotes circulation and, in conjunction with correct work, will help to develop muscular condition. It must be remembered that the skin is a gland of equal importance to other glands within the body. It provides the means for the body to rid itself of toxic residues and to control temperature. A popular song of some years ago proclaimed that 'everybody needs skin to keep their insides in'! In fact, it has a far more important function. Pores must be kept open, scurf eliminated and sources of natural oils given free access to the coat. A clean skin will promote general health and grooming is therefore far more important than its mere cosmetic value, although a gleaming coat is in itself proof that the horse is healthy and capable of fulfilling its potential. Grooming with an electric rotary brush groomer

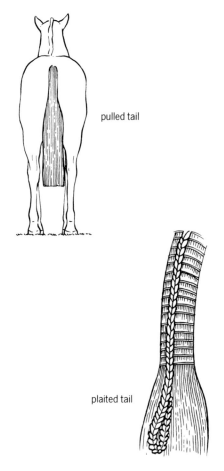

pulled tail

plaited tail

Plaited and pulled tail

first, to lift the dirt and massage the muscles, followed by a good hand grooming will take about an hour. We prefer massaging the muscles rather than strapping as the action of 'banging' the muscle can break down as much of the muscle tissue as you hope to build up by the contraction of the muscle as you hit it.

The horse must also be kept properly trimmed and have its mane pulled. This will enable it to be neatly plaited for competitions, which is important for turnout.

I keep a hood on my horse at night, which means the mane can be pulled quite short but will still lie flat. The tail should either be neatly pulled or left full and plaited for competition. If the horse is to be turned out for extended periods, especially in adverse weather, it may be better to consider plaiting rather than pulling the tail. With the stabled horse, protection of the dock area becomes less important and a pulled tail becomes preferable to a plaited tail. If it is pulled, a tail bandage must be put on each day to ensure that the hairs lie flat.

The decision of whether to clip or not is up to the individual owner. I usually keep my horses fully clipped all the year round. In the summer they do not look bald but it keeps the coat very short. It necessitates keeping them rugged up, of course, but it also means that they sweat less in work and therefore take less out of themselves. As well as a thorough grooming each day, the horse should be washed down after fast work. In the summer this will cause no problem and it can be walked to dry off quickly. In winter, only wipe the sweaty areas off quickly and put a sweat rug on with a rug on top to keep the horse warm while it is drying off. The horse must not be allowed to get cold as it will then catch a chill.

The use of an ordinary bed sheet, next to the horse, under the rugs, will greatly reduce the need to dry clean the rugs. An ordinary bed sheet can easily be put into a washing machine or launderette and can be changed weekly, ensuring that dirt does not build up in the clothing. Always add extra clothing in preference to closing windows or top doors. The optimum is to provide bodily warmth and maximum fresh air, which is best achieved by additional clothing and the maintenance of a fresh air flow.

I would stress the importance of having a good farrier, keeping vaccinations up to date and the routine tasks of a correct worming and teeth-rasping programme.

FEEDING

To be successful, feeding must be adjusted to the individual needs of the particular horse. The basic needs are universal; the peripheral requirements are individual. Observations made by the keeper as to the tastes, veterinary priorities, temperamental needs and work load of the animal concerned are important. The golden rules of feeding have stood the test of time and can now be backed up with scientific knowledge.

Good quality hay is essential. I have found that horses that are on a high intake of concentrates prefer good quality meadow hay rather than good

The Golden Rules of Feeding

U Feed little and often – because of the small size of the horse's stomach and the length of its intestine. Remember the horse is designed to be a trickle feeder, eating a little and moving on.

U Feed according to type and work done – Thoroughbred types will not usually require so much heating food as this may have an alcoholic effect on them, a coarser-bred horse may need to be given extra energy. They all require a balanced diet to work hard and keep their bodies in good condition.

U Feed plenty of bulk to aid digestion.

U Water before feeding so that the food is not washed through the system too quickly before it is properly digested.

U Feed good quality food – it is a false economy to do anything else.

U Feed at regular times – routine is vital to the well being of the horse. It must be able to anticipate when it is going to have its next feed so that it will not have a reason to become anxious. Anxiety will cause loss of condition through stress and may lead to the development of stable vices.

U Feed something succulent every day to replace the absence of grass. This will keep a horse interested in its diet.

U Keep feeding utensils scrupulously clean – sour, stale food will put the horse off its feed quicker than anything.

Never re-offer a discarded feed for economic reasons. It is better to 'waste' a refused feed than attempt to force the horse to accept it through hunger. To the human the feed may be perfectly acceptable. The horse may have detected sourness, mouse fouling or other unpalatable elements that would not be discerned by the human nose. Remember the occasions upon which you have rejected a meal which, on face value, seemed entirely acceptable. Allow your horse the same freedom of choice.

U Feed the horse as an individual. Some horses will need as little as 4.5 kg (10 lb) of concentrate per day; others will require 7–8 kg (16–18 lb). Increase the nutritional value of the food to match the physical demands made on the horse. Cut down the concentrates whenever work is reduced. Temperament must always be taken into account when the amount of concentrates are being calculated. Some people can get giggly on half a pint of lager while others can drink half a pint of Scotch and still seem sober! Some horses can take quantities of oats; others make do with the smell!

quality seed hay. We have always been brought up to believe that horses in fast work must have seed hay but the horse is really the only one to tell us which is best for it!

Horses very often go off their feed as they approach peak fitness and can become very finicky eaters. It is most alarming for any caring owner when their pride and joy stops eating! If your horse eats better at night, give it an extra feed late in the evening. If it will not eat until after it has worked, give it its breakfast after it has worked. The most important thing is to get to know your horse and pander (to a certain extent!) to its preferences. Do not regulate your feeding routine to fit in with your own convenience. The object of the whole exercise is to make sure that the horse receives the necessary fuel for the job in hand. Some people eat their main meal in the middle of the day and have a light supper. Others reverse the process; others still put their faith in a full breakfast. Whatever suits your horse should become your routine. This can become difficult if several horses with different needs are kept in one yard. The successful trainer will find solutions to this problem by recognising in the first place that there is a problem, and in the second place allowing for individual preferences. It is quite common for a horse to leave its breakfast on the morning of a competition.

WATER

In particularly hot and humid weather the horse will recover quickly from strenuous work if electrolyte salts are added to the drinking water. If two buckets of water are made available to the horse, one containing electrolytes and the other not, the horse can then drink them if it requires them. It is a good idea to introduce these salts after work at home so that the horse will then drink them after a competition. For full information on the type and amount to be given, consult your veterinary surgeon.

The horse should have access to water all the time in the stable but if you travel to the event on the morning of the competition do not allow the horse to have a long drink just before the cross-country. Offer it a drink when you first arrive and at frequent periods during the day, especially if it is hot. Usually, the horse will take just a couple of sips at a time. It is important that the horse continues to consume some water if it is hot, to prevent it from becoming dehydrated. The experts in long-distance riding have done a lot of research into how much water horses should consume while working. Obviously, they should not have a large drink of water just before galloping, but frequent small amounts are essential.

ROUTINE

Routine is important to all horses but it is equally important that your horse becomes accustomed to working at any time of the day or evening. It must not refuse to co-operate if it is asked to perform a dressage test at 2 pm in the afternoon simply because you always ride at 7 am in the morning before you go to work. It is

Canter upsides

also beneficial to make the horse work in different situations and to teach it to ignore neighbouring distractions. Sometimes make it do a dressage test where it is used to cantering and *vice versa*.

VARIETY

It is important that horses are given plenty of variety in their work. Hacking out using as many different routes as possible, integrated with schooling, jump training and fast work, will help to stimulate interest. The fast work is best done on its own if the horse is excitable but if it is stuffy it will help to develop the ability to gallop if it goes out with a companion. Hunting or drag hunting may also stimulate interest. Of the two, the latter is probably the better teaching aid. The route is preordained and dangers should be reduced to a minimum. Provided the organisers of the drag are sensible, the track will be fair, straightforward but varied. The route followed by the true hunt is unpredictable and may include unforeseen hazards such as farm machinery on the landing side of jumps, atrocious going or unsuitable or downright dangerous obstacles. As good horses are now so expensive, I do not think it is worth the risk involved. There are now so many professionally prepared courses where the atmosphere of hunting can be simulated safely by having two or three horses to follow over a variety of fences that the danger of being kicked, barged into and crossed over while tackling unseen obstacles is totally unwarranted.

GENERAL RULES

Some general rules should be observed while training your horse at home. When out hacking, remember that the horse must not slop along as you enjoy the countryside. It must always be working and even when it is given a long rein while walking, it must maintain a marching rhythm as it stretches the muscles in its neck and topline.

The ground on which you are working must be taken into account. Trotting along the road must be done at a slow speed while being energetic enough to prevent unnecessary concussion. Hard, hard hammering down the road is detrimental but a sustained, controlled, steady trot on a hard surface is therapeutic as it will help to toughen tendons and ligaments in the leg, develop the expansion of the frog and stimulate circulation within the foot. Grass may be slippery in dry weather. In wet weather it may be deep. In uncultivated areas, twitch grass can cover concrete and other unyielding surfaces. On one occasion my mother circled on what appeared to be a grass-covered area but which turned out to be the foundations of a former aerodrome hut. The horse losts its balance and my mother broke her ankle as a result. Sand can be very hard, causing stress fractures if galloped on without first being harrowed.

The horse must always be well warmed up before doing strenuous work and cooled down slowly afterwards to prevent unnecessary strain being put onto the lungs, heart and tendons. A period of walking after fast work will also prevent a

Washing down is essential in hot/humid conditions

build up of lactic acid in the muscles, which causes azoturia, a cramping affliction of the muscles in the loins, which can become chronic.

Weather conditions also play a great part in the preparation of the event horse. Humid conditions require special care as the ability of the skin to perspire freely is inhibited by the humidity of the atmosphere. Wash the horse down and put plenty of cool water or ice packs between the ears and the hindlegs to cool the main arteries quickly. Bad weather or very hard conditions may necessitate the use of all-weather gallops for your fast training work.

The horse must be thoroughly checked over each morning and evening. Its legs must always be checked after work, especially fast

work, and again in the evening. Any filling or heat must be reduced immediately before continuing with any canter work. Several types of cooling lotions or jellies are sold for application after fast work and they are advantageous in many cases. However, a hosepipe can not only be the most efficacious, but is definitely the cheapest, means of reducing inflammation and swelling. Do not forget to grease the heel before applying the water to the leg.

Any minute change in the horse's temperament, attitude to work or feeding must be recorded and alterations made to remedy the situation. When the horse is fully fit, with careful attention to feeding and exercise it will be able to retain its fitness for about twelve weeks.

A Blood Test

A blood test can be taken for a number of reasons but it is useful to have one taken when the horse first comes into work. This can tell you if it is anaemic. Anaemia is as common in horses as it is in humans and, obviously, the horse will lack energy if it is anaemic. Blood testing can be done for worms as well. Another test can be done as you anticipate that your horse is approaching full fitness so that you can be absolutely sure all is well.

SUMMARY

1. Good basic stable management is essential at all times.

2. We must be fully aware of the horse's natural instincts and way of life when we try to domesticiate it.

3. Feed according to the established rules of feeding which have stood the test of time and are now backed up with scientific knowledge.

4. Variety will help to keep the horse happy and fresh in its work.

5. The horse must be well warmed up before being asked to work strenuously.

6. Humid conditions require the horse to receive special care.

7. The horse must be thoroughly checked for injuries and strains after work and each morning and evening.

CHAPTER SEVEN

PREPARING FOR COMPETITION

The routine and work should not be changed but do not give the horse strenuous work as it requires about four days to recover fully from a complete work out. Feeding during the day also remains the same except that the hay ration should be reduced to approximately 4.5 kg (10 lb) in the evening. If straw is the only available bedding, it will be necessary to put a muzzle on the horse to prevent it from eating this. The preferable alternative, should it be available, is habitually to bed the horse on shavings or shredded paper. There must be access to water all the time.

It is advisable to try to walk the course the day before the competition so that you have as much time as you need to make a careful inspection. It also enables you to 'sleep on' any problems and have another look at the course in the morning. The feasibility of this will depend upon the distance of the event and also the time that is available. If you have already had time away from work to compete, it may not be possible to have extra time off the day before. If you do manage to travel the day before and stay overnight, it will be possible to walk the course and also to work your horse in the vicinity of the arena where the dressage will be held the following day.

Whenever you decide to travel, have a checklist already prepared and as you load the different items, tick them off so that nothing is left behind.

PLAITING

If you are leaving early the following morning for the event, it may be necessary to plait the horse the night before. This is not a practice to encourage as it must be like sleeping with rollers in for the horse! Also, most horses know that something exciting is about to happen as soon as their mane or tail is plaited and may then not settle and rest as they should, which usually means that their breakfast will be rejected! To avoid this apprehension on the horse's part, it can be beneficial to practise plaiting during quiet periods of training so that the process is not associated entirely with high days of competition and excitement.

If it is decided to plait the evening before, the plaits must be covered once they are completed to prevent them becoming filled with straw or shavings. A leg from a pair of ladies' tights, laid down the neck with a rubber band securing each plait, will keep them clean. If you use a hood on your horse in the stable this will also

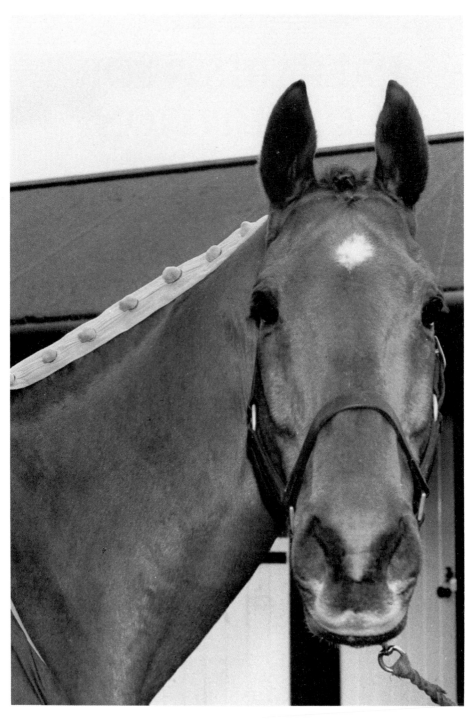

The leg of a pair of ladies tights over a row of plaits will keep them clean and tidy

keep them clean and neat. A tail bandage and stocking need to be put over a plaited tail.

TRANSPORT

Always load the vehicle the night before to reduce the number of jobs to be done before leaving in the morning. It may be advisable to leave valuable items in the tackroom to prevent theft, but have them properly cleaned and ready to load.

The lorry or towing vehicle and trailer must be thoroughly checked. Regular servicing of all vehicles is essential to reduce the chance of unnecessary breakdowns. All hinges must be well oiled so that the ramp is easily lifted and secured. Before putting bedding on the floor make sure it does not show any wear. Wooden floors get damp and can then rot. For this reason, it is essential that dirty bedding is mucked out and clean bedding lifted off the damp areas after each outing.

Obviously, the fuel tank needs to be full of petrol/diesel and the levels of the water and oil must be topped up. The lights and indicators must also be in proper working order. It is especially important that they are checked from behind in the case of a trailer as there may be a break in the connection so that the lights do not operate. For the comfort of the horse and ease of driving, always make sure the tyres are at the correct pressure.

CHECK LIST FOR A ONE-DAY EVENT

A haynet – to travel inside but not to be given to the horse on the outward journey. When the horse has finished and has cooled down it can be given. The practice of hanging the haynets on the outside of the ramp where they become covered in dirt and dust off the road and get filled with exhaust fumes is to be discouraged. If they have to be put inside the towing vehicle, travel them in a large plastic bag to prevent any mess.

Water carrier and buckets – in hot weather more than one carrier may be necessary. As mentioned before, the horse should be encouraged to drink small amounts of water at regular intervals, especially in humid conditions. It will also need liberal washing down when it has finished – unless it is bitterly cold which may be likely early in the season.

Feed – if the horse will eat at a competition and it has finished early, it can have a feed. This can be brought ready prepared so it need only be dampened.

Electrolyte salts – for the drinking water when the horse has finished.

Grooming kit – to include extra washing-down sponges

77

and a sweat scraper, hoof oil, Vaseline and fly repellent. Horses that have respiratory problems after travelling will benefit from having a little Vick put up their nostrils. Spare plaiting kit for any running repairs and studs with the fitting key. The stud holes should be well cleaned out, oiled and filled with either small road studs or cotton wool to allow easy fitting the following day. Grease for application to the horse's legs before going cross-country. This should be of a non-toxic nature: grease as used in the motor industry is toxic, lanoline is not.

Rugs – a sweat rug and a spare travelling rug in case one becomes damp.

Bandages/ boots – travelling bandages and gamgee for the return journey when the horse is tired and its legs require more support. Boots or bandages for competing with adhesive tape/ sewing equipment and scissors. Over-reach boots.

Tack – saddle and bridle. Spare bridle if you have one but spare reins, girths and stirrup leathers are essential. Any secondary bits if they are used. Martingale or breastplate

and attachment. Surcingle.

Lungeing equipment – cavesson headcollar, side reins, lunge rein and whip.

First aid kit – for horse and rider. All events will have a vet and doctor present but it is advisable to have some cotton wool, salt and some wound powder/ spray so that you can treat minor wounds. Animalintex poultice is a useful standby. Some plasters and aspirin can be handy for the rider. For anything that is more than minor, seek professional advice.

Rider – jacket, boots, breeches. I always take a spare pair of breeches in case the weather is bad and they get wet or I have a fall! Wet breeches on a wet saddle create a very unsafe and uncomfortable feeling! Number bib, medical card holder, hat, hairnet, gloves, stick, spurs and a change of clothes to travel home in.

Passport – I have left this until last as it is essential. My horse's passport lives in the lorry so that I cannot forget it. At affiliated competitions you are *not* allowed to compete without one and it can be asked for at any time. If you are away overnight, you will not be allowed into the stabling without it.

Overnight Extras

Stable tools – fork, brush, skip and muck sack.
Bedding – it is usually provided but you may have to bring your own shavings/paper.
Buckets and feed bowl – two buckets.
Feed – usual concentrate feed plus any additives that are normally fed.
Hay
Tack cleaning and boot cleaning equipment.
Night rugs and blankets.

Always remember that if you are staying away overnight you are the guest of someone else, so always leave your stable and the space outside as clean and tidy as you would like them to be left in your yard at home. Often stables are left in a disgraceful condition and that only brings our sport into disrepute.

STARTING TIMES

The exact starting times for each competitor are available the evening before the event. They are obtained by telephoning the number stated on the schedule within specified times. For BHS affiliated horse trials, you will receive back part of your entry form with your section and number for the day filled in beside the name of your horse as confirmation of your entry. It is necessary to quote this information when you ring for your times.

The times you are given are strictly adhered to unless there has been an unavoidable incident which could not be foreseen. It is your responsibility to be at the right place at the right time with all the correct equipment. Having got your times, write them down on a piece of paper or card and put them somewhere *safe*. I used to write mine first on the schedule and then on a piece of card stuck on the inside of the lorry cab glass. This meant that everyone could see them and it was especially useful if there was more than one horse running. Your whole day will revolve around these times.

SUMMARY

1. Do as many of the jobs for the following morning as possible on the day before the event.
2. Transport must always be thoroughly serviced anyway and then final checks made before a journey.
3. Make a checklist before loading the equipment so that nothing gets left behind.
4. Never forget the horse's passport.
5. Extra equipment must be taken when staying away overnight.
6. The exact starting times for each competitor are available the evening before the competition.

CHAPTER EIGHT

ON THE DAY

AN EARLY START

As mentioned in the previous chapter you will by now know exactly when you are to compete so you can work out a plan to make sure the day runs smoothly. In my experience it is always better to leave a little extra time than to have to rush. This is when tempers become frayed and horses go badly!

Work your day back from the first time you have been given, which is for the dressage. If you need 45 minutes to ride in before the test, add some extra time to ride from the lorry park to the working-in areas, so making that one hour. You will need time to remove all your horse's travelling kit, brush it over, put the studs in, put hoof oil and quarter marks on and the saddle and bridle. You also need to get dressed in your smart clothes and number bib. All this will take about half an hour if you have help but probably nearer an hour if you do not. I always like to titivate and saddle my own horse but then I like someone to lunge it for me while I titivate myself!

If you have not walked the cross-country and/or show jumping courses the previous day, time for this has to be allowed also. Even if there will be time after you have ridden your dressage, I would advise you to walk the courses in the early morning.

A rough guide for a dressage time of 12.15 pm, including walking the courses, would be:

5.30 am	Water, feed.
5.45 am	Muck out and tidy yard.
6.15 am	Groom, plait and dress horse for the journey.
7.00 am	Change, cup of coffee and toast.
7.15 am	Load the horse and any last-minute things.
7.30 am	Leave (for journey of, say, 80 km or 50 miles).
9.00 am	Arrive at the horse trials. Check the horse. Lower the ramp.
9.15 am	Collect your number and programme. Walk the courses.
11.00 am	Brush horse over, put studs in and saddle the horse.
11.15 am	Lunge/change.
11.30 am	Mount and ride in.
12.15 am	Dressage test.

Once you have started your day the time rushes by and there are always scores to be assessed. Certain fences may be causing problems. Time should be allowed to observe what these problems are – as long as you

All courses must be walked properly with the distances carefully measured

are not one of the unfortunates going early and revealing the problems. It is better to walk the cross-country course before there are horses jumping it so that the distances and problems can be carefully scrutinised. Normally a Novice cross-country course can be walked in about an hour with an extra half hour for the show jumping.

Before setting out on the walk round, a programme must be bought and your number collected from the secretary. The programme will have a map of the course with a description of each fence, the length of the course, the optimum time and the time allowed. It may also have illustrations of the obstacles, in which case the flagging must be studied before deciding which option

you wish to take.

The next calculation is how long the journey will take. The transporting of horses must be done carefully and relatively slowly. Horseboxes can usually be driven a little faster than trailers but it must be remembered that horses can still become frightened and/or injured if driven too fast. No exact speed limits can be put on horse transport as the type of road, the road surface, weather conditions, the number of hills and the age and condition of the vehicle all have to be taken into consideration, but about 60 kmph (40 mph) is probably the maximum on good roads.

Your morning routine also has to be accurately provided for. This will obviously alter as to whether you only have the one horse that is competing or others that also have to be looked after before you can leave.

Obviously, walking the courses the day before will leave more time for you on the day and the start of everything may not need to be so early. On the other hand, if the dressage time is earlier, it may be necessary to get up even earlier. Alternatives can be made within the plan to fit individual requirements. The main things that cannot and should not be skimped on are the travelling time needed to get to the competition, walking of the courses and the riding in for the dressage. Individual horses will require more or less time for the riding in, depending on their temperament or physical ability.

CLOTHING

When travelling the horse the rules of good stable management still

Horse dressed for travelling in a modern rug and boots.

apply. It must be kept warm in cold weather and cool in summer, have plenty of fresh air but no draughts and a non-slippery floor to stand on. In my experience most horses travel well if they are suitably clothed and are driven considerably.

Rugs

When deciding on the amount of rugs to put on, first consider the weather conditions and the type of vehicle you are using. A horsebox will always be warmer than a trailer and several horses will always be warmer than one on its own. Nowadays there are several types of combined sweat and day rugs. These are ideal as if the horse does sweat, the rug allows the moisture to escape but also keeps the horse dry. Certain makes are thicker than others and are therefore more suitable for the winter months. In very severe cold an extra rug or blanket may be necessary, especially in a trailer. It is important that the horse is kept as warm while it is travelling as it is in its stable at home.

During the summer a lightweight sweat rug-combined day sheet or just a day sheet will probably be enough. The time of day that you expect to travel must also be taken into consideration. The early morning can often be cold and damp while later it can become stifflingly hot. On days like this, your horse will need more rugs for the outward journey than the return. It is advisable to take a spare rug in case the horse sweats or it rains and the rugs get wet. If your horse tends to sweat while travelling and you do not have a combined rug, it is advisable to put a sweat rug on with another rug on top, with the corners

turned back at the shoulders, secured by a roller.

Bandages/Boots

The horse's legs must be protected while travelling. This can be done either with bandages and knee and hock boots or by boots that cover the leg from above the knee and hock to the coronet. The all-in-one boots are quick and easy to put on and take off and offer good protection but no support. For this reason I always travel my horse with bandages and Fibagee on the return journey. If the horse has just completed a long and arduous day I think it requires some support on its legs. Knee and hock boots will offer protection for the knees and hocks. The top strap must be firmly secured but the lower strap must be loose, preferably on the last hole, so as not to restrict the tendons. The tail must always have a tail bandage and if travelling with a partition or ramp immediately behind the horse, a tail guard will be necessary over the bandage to prevent rubbing. If you are using a tail guard, it will be necessary to have an extra roller or surcingle over the rug to which it can be attached. Most modern designs of rugs have surcingles stitched to them so it is impossible to secure a tail guard to them without an additional surcingle or roller.

Headcollar

A leather headcollar with a lead rope is also advisable. In the event of an accident, this will break, whereas a nylon one will not. If the horse is very tall a poll guard may also be

necessary. They come in two types:
1. A pad like a sausage which fits onto the headpiece of the headcollar.
2. A skull cap which fits over the top of the head allowing the ears through two extra holes.

Some horses, especially young horses or stallions, may need tying to a chain in the transport to prevent escape. If a chain is used, it should be attached to the ring by string so that there is a quick release system in an emergency. The horse should *never* be led on a chain – always use a rope.

It is also not advisable to travel horses with jump studs in their shoes as they can tread on themselves or each other.

LOADING THE HORSE
This does not usually present any problems with an experienced owner and an experienced horse. A young or nervous horse must have plenty of practice in loading so that it will load easily and confidently on the day of the competition.

Put the lorry or trailer alongside a building or wall to help keep the horse straight. The ramp should not be too steep but must be firm. It may be necessary to insert a chock under one side if the ground is uneven.

The transport should have been prepared for the journey the evening before. The horse should be led from the nearside and taken straight to the ramp of the vehicle with the leader looking straight ahead, never at the horse. Have an assistant standing near the ramp so that when the horse is safely inside the breeching strap, in the case of a trailer, or the partition

in the case of a lorry, can be secured. The ramp must then be put up – in the case of a trailer as quickly as possible to prevent the horse trying to back out. The horse can then be tied up. Do not start to go under the breast bar or do anything that may startle the horse until it is safely in and the ramp is up, because its immediate defence will be to pull back. Go out of the side, groom's door.

Leading a horse without help is a little more difficult. Putting a horse into a lorry does not cause too much of a problem, although it is sensible to tie it up to a piece of string attached to the tie-ring before adjusting the partition. A trailer is a little more difficult. The easiest way is to attach a lunge rein to the headcollar and thread it through the tie ring before coming back to the horse. Gently pull the lunge rein as you put your hand on the horse's hindquarters. 'An old hand' may prefer to walk itself into the trailer so that you can attach the breeching straps and fix the ramp and then tie it up.

Horses that are reluctant to load must have the reason for the reluctance established and then resolved. The secret of successful loading is to have plenty of time, both for the loading process and the journey. If the horse is strong, always load it with a bridle on instead of a headcollar so that it does not get into the habit of running off in the opposite direction! In the early stages with a reluctant loader, a lunge rein attached to the uprights on either side of the ramp can be used. As the horse moves forward, so the lunge reins are crossed behind it, 'squeezing the horse' up the ramp and

Whenever possible have an assistant to help when loading a horse

preventing the quarters from swinging from side to side. This method is obviously only possible when two assistants are available to manipulate the lunge reins.

The handler must wear suitable non-slip shoes and gloves for leading and loading the horse. Remember that a firm attitude, with a quiet, encouraging voice, and an organised approach will load most horses successfully.

For a short journey of up to three hours, a quick check of the horse and possibly the offer of some water is all that will be required. If you are travelling the day before the competition the horse may appreciate a haynet en route. Obviously, the longer the journey, especially in warm weather, the more often it will be necessary to stop and offer the horse some water. During the journey always be ready to stop and check any suspicious noises or movements in the back. A quick stop can often prevent a stressful situation building up for your passenger!

SUMMARY

1. Leaving plenty of time for preparation and reconnaissance will enhance the chances of success.
2. Work backwards from the first starting time and make yourself a rough plan of when you are going to do everything.
3. The horse must be properly protected during travelling.
4. When deciding what your horse should wear take into consideration:

a) the weather conditions;
b) the type of transport;
c) the length of the journey;
d) whether the horse is on its own or with others.

5. Practise loading your horse before the day of the horse trials so that there are no hiccups over loading.
6. When choosing a site for loading, make sure that it will assist in obtaining a successful conclusion.
7. Always check unusual noises, movements or smells that may occur during the journey.

CHAPTER NINE

AT THE HORSE TRIALS

ARRIVAL

As you approach the location of the horse trials, look out for the directional signs. It is important that you co-operate with the organisers and park in the appropriate place. Having lowered the ramp and checked the horses, get your bearings and go to the secretary. From him or her you will collect your number and programme. If you have not walked the two courses previously, now is the time to do so. If you have previously walked and are undecided about the problems of a particular obstacle, now is the time to go and inspect it again and make your decision. It is important that you have a clear picture of the fences and the route that you are taking in your mind's eye before you start out on the cross-

Collecting numbers, buying a programme and checking the starting times

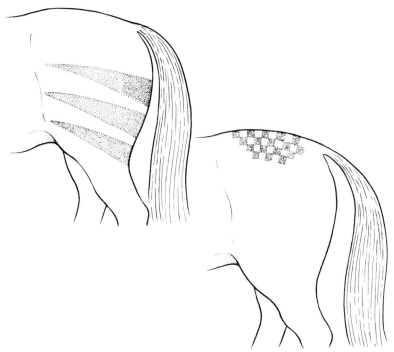

Quarter marks can be put onto the horse's hindquarters

country. It will be advantageous to watch a couple of competitors before your turn in the show jumping in case you have a momentary loss of memory!

I cannot overstress how important it is for you to have a companion at an event. To have someone who can double-up as a groom and possibly a driver is a bonus.

DRESSAGE

For the dressage phase the horse must be clean, smart and plaited. It will need a snaffle bridle (for Novice standard although a double bridle can be used at Intermediate standard and above) and a saddle. If required, the horse can wear a hunter breastplate and if the ground is slippery it may need studs. After the studs have been

fitted, the hoof oil can be applied. A little Vaseline or baby oil around the eyes, muzzle and dock region will give the skin a gloss. In hot weather fly spray may be needed. A lot of horses do not like the noise of the spray, in which case apply it with a cloth. Quarter marks can be put on the hindquarters with a body brush or tail comb to show off the horse's quarters.

As I have mentioned I like my horse to have a few minutes on the lunge so that it can relax and have a look around before I mount. If my companion or groom can lunge, I leave them to it while I go and get dressed in beige jodpurs, black boots, stock or tie, jacket and hat and find my gloves and schooling stick. If this routine is not possible, I lunge my horse first then tie it up in the box while I get ready. My riding in for the dressage will follow a similar routine to my riding at home. Basically it is to supple and loosen the horse's muscles, establish balance and rhythm and get it obedient to the aids. Before starting the warm-up routine do check with the dressage steward that things are running to time. Occasionally the times run late if there has been a hold-up, which means you will have some extra time. If, on the other hand they are ahead of time, there is no reason for you to enter the arena before your allotted time, so do not be rushed.

About ten minutes before you are due to enter, get your helper to re-oil the horse's hooves and wipe the horse over either with a brush or a cloth damped with baby oil (carefully missing the quarter marks). Finally, a quick rub over the rider's boots with a duster will give the perfect finishing touch!

The horse can be offered a small drink when it has finished the dressage test and returned to the lorry – more of a mouthwash than a quaff.

SHOW JUMPING

The plaits can be removed for the show jumping phase but generally they are left in as they improve the horse's appearance. In the past there was a school of thought which held that plaiting the horse's mane restricted the movement of head and

Lungeing the horse before the dressage will help it to relax

neck. This theory has now largely been discounted and many international show jumpers compete in the ring with plaited manes. If they are removed, always leave the first one, behind the ears, in for the cross-country, to stitch the headpiece to.

The horse must have the appropriate bridle and, if required, a martingale fitted. If leather reins have been used for the dressage, they need to be changed, either for rubber-covered or continental web reins. A numnah and jumping saddle with a surcingle are also basic requirements.

Horses always react to the way their rider is feeling so be very careful to remain relaxed throughout the warm-up and test period. The most common saying heard as competitors leave the area is 'He worked in so well but when he got into the arena . . .!' A fit horse is even more sensitive than normal so do not let your own tensions transmit themselves to the horse. On the other hand, the most impressive test may often be produced when you are sitting on a 'time-bomb'. The trick is to avoid the actual explosion.

Warm-up

Before entering the dressage arena it is important that the horse is really relaxed – touching on being bored. It must be willing to go forward but still be obedient to the aids, and the ways to achieve this are many. Some riders lunge their horses before they start working them; some work their horses for a period of time and then rest them, starting again a short time before they enter the arena. Whatever form the warm-up period takes, the essential common

denominator is to leave sufficient time so that horse and rider are fully relaxed and supple but the horse still retains its spontaneity and gaiety of performance.

Tendon or brushing boots should afford enough protection for the show jumping phase. It is also advisable to use over-reach boots while jumping. If studs have not been used for the dressage, it may be necessary to fit them before jumping.

The rider stays in the same clothes as for the dressage except that if you have worn a hunting cap, it must now be changed for a crash helmet for both phases of jumping. For the show jumping phase a dark blue or black silk must be worn.

Riding In

This should be limited to limbering up as your main warming up has been done prior to the dressage. Do not overjump the practice fences. Remember that one of the most important reasons for using the practice fence is to build the horse's confidence. Too often one sees precisely the opposite as a result of overjumping and the consequent destruction of confidence in both horse and rider.

A small amount of water can be offered to the horse when it has finished but this should be limited if the cross-country start is imminent.

CROSS-COUNTRY

The horse must wear boots or bandages on its legs. Boots must be strong and supple but not too heavy or absorbent. Bandages must be put on with great care. They must be used

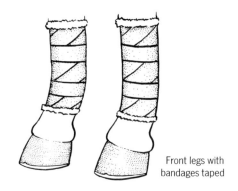

Front legs with
bandages taped

Bandages must be securely fastened

with either gamgee or some other
form of protection underneath so as
not to cause constriction or uneven
pressure. Bandages must always be
secured by sewing or adhesive tape.
Sewing can be difficult if the horse is
fidgety and will not stand still, and
especially difficult to undo later when
it returns with the stitches covered in
mud! If you use tape, always be
especially careful with the tension as
it must not be any tighter than the
bandage. The over-reach boots will
already be fitted for the show
jumping. Any adjustments required
must also be made to the bridle.
Grease can be applied to the chest,
forearms and from the stifle to the
front of the hock joint of the horse.
This makes it easier for it to slide over
an obstacle if it hits it hard.

The rider will exchange their
jacket for a brightly coloured back
protector or plain back protector with
a coloured jumper over the top. The
cover on the crash cap may also be
changed.

Again, riding in for this phase
should consist of only a short canter
and a couple of jumps. The steward

will give you a warning as the
competitor before you starts and then
count you down from fifteen seconds
in the starting box. Enter the box at
about six seconds so that you can
walk a small circle and do not stand
still for too long. An excitable horse
may need someone to lead it into the
box.

At the finish of the cross-country,
the horse should be allowed to reduce
speed slowly to prevent tired tendons
being injured by sudden changes of
speed or direction. As the horse walks
the rider must dismount but keep the
horse walking. The helper must then
loosen the girth, surcingle and
noseband while on the move. On
cool days a sweat rug should then be
thrown over the horse to prevent it
catching a cold.

CARE OF THE HORSE AFTER IT HAS FINISHED

On returning to the lorry, remove the
tack and cover the horse with a sweat
rug in the shade in the summer to
prevent burning, or a heavier rug if
the weather is cool. Offer the horse a
small drink of chilled water (i.e.
water with the chill taken off). We
use the scale of five sips every five
minutes and continue walking until
the horse's breathing has returned to
normal. If the horse is used to
electrolyte salts in its water at home,
use them at the competition to aid
recovery. Offer plain water also.

When the horse is back to normal
remove all boots and/or bandages and
studs, wash it down thoroughly and
check for injuries. Remove excess
water with a sweat scraper and cover
the horse with a sweat rug. From this

time it can have about half a bucket of water every fifteen minutes. Rub the legs with a cooling gel and walk the horse until it is dry.

If the horse recovers quickly, it can be offered a haynet in the lorry and allowed to stand and relax. Later, it can be offered more water and a small feed and have its legs bandaged.

In very hot conditions, immediately the horse has finished lead it around and then wash down and continue leading it around. Repeat the washing down and walking process until the temperature, pulse and respiration rates are all back to normal. Ice packs can be put between the ears and iced water used on the underside of the neck, the front legs and the inside of the hindlegs. Avoid the loins and hindquarters. Give water as directed above to prevent dehydration.

If you are lucky enough to be in the prize giving, it is important to be available on time and properly turned out. Riders must be dressed as for the dressage phase, with breeches, boots, tie or stock, jacket and hat. Without the support of several generous sponsors and the dedicated work of numerous voluntary helpers, horse trials could not exist, so the least competitors can do is to turn themselves out smartly for the finale of the day – the prize giving. A quick word of thanks also does not cost anything but means a lot to the organisers.

On returning to the lorry, check that the horse is comfortable, offer it more water and start the journey home.

When you arrive home, put the horse in the stable with plenty of water and a haynet. Remove its travelling equipment and brush it over, checking again for any injuries. Rebandage the legs with dry bandages over a cooling lotion or cold kaolin and put the night rugs on. Feed the horse its normal amount of feed. If it seems really exhausted, offer a bran mash instead.

Make a late-night check on the hay and water and to see if the horse has finished its feed. It should also be resting quietly and comfortably.

The next day, carry on stable duties as normal. Remove the bandages and hose off any kaolin. Check that the horse is sound by trotting it up. Lead it out in hand or turn it out in a small paddock for half an hour to loosen its muscles. Give it a thorough grooming and leave it to rest while you start the marathon job of cleaning all your equipment.

SUMMARY

1. Turnout is of the utmost importance throughout the competition.
2. The horse must have a saddle and snaffle bridle (for Novice events) and if required a breast plate and studs for the dressage.
3. The rider must wear beige breeches, black boots, tie or stock, jacket, hat and pale gloves.
4. Riding in for the dressage will follow a similar pattern as is used at home.
5. The horse can have boots or bandages for the show jumping and any changes that are necessary made to the saddle and bridle. The rider must dress

as for dressage but have a crash helmet with a dark cover.

6. The riding in and jumping of the practice fence must not be overdone.

7. The horse's equipment can remain the same for the cross-country but the rider must wear a back protector. It is usual to exchange the jacket for a jersey or coloured body protector.

8. On the return from the cross-country, the horse must be kept walking, offered water little and often and washed down.

9. Ice packs and cold water can be used in extremely hot weather to cool the horse.

10. Respect the sponsors and organisers by going to the prize giving well turned out.

11. Put travelling bandages on the horse for the journey home.

12. Keep checking that the horse is relaxed and comfortable when you get home.

EPILOGUE

There is no short cut to fitness. The recipe is always the same, the ingredients unchanged. Take sufficient quantities of good food and add plenty of suitable exercise. Supply these for a considerable period of time and garnish with daily grooming of a vigorous nature. Put the whole mixture into a regular stable routine and good condition will, in the course of time, appear. The more energetic and exacting the work, the longer must be the time allowed to attain the necessary degree of fitness. Time is absolutely essential. Time for fat to be absorbed, for muscle to develop; time for heart and lungs to grow strong and equal to the tasks set; time for tendons and joints, through gradually increasing demands, to grow capable of withstanding both prolonged strain and the sudden shock encountered in emergencies. Above all, time must be allowed for the internal structures of the horse to come to a peak of efficiency in their functions so that fatigue may be kept at bay. It is foolhardy and the worst possible horsemanship to work an overtired, unfit horse, for it is then that accidents occur: strains, maybe of a lasting nature, are caused or bones are broken. Once good hard condition has been obtained, judicious work and exercise, plus the other ingredients mentioned, will not only maintain that condition, but will add to it, so that the horse becomes able to perform its work more and more efficiently and is less prone to accident or disease.

Experience the enjoyment of training and preparation for horse trials. Experience the enjoyment of competition. Above all experience the enjoyment of riding a horse completely trained for eventing. It is essential for the horse to share these enjoyments too, because eventing is a partnership involving horse and rider.

INDEX

Page numbers in *italics* indicate a figure
appearing on a different page to its text.